D0365243

y

E

v. 1-94

CHICAGO PUBLIC LIBRARY

FORM 19

Empire Builders

More Praise for *Empire Builders*

Burt Folsom is one of the most exciting and dynamic historians writing today. In *Empire Builders,* he brings history gloriously alive. He also thoroughly and effectively demolishes the revisionist myth that our early entrepreneurs were 'robber barons.' I give this book four stars.

George Roche
President, Hillsdale College

Empire Builders is a great read. I thoroughly enjoyed it even when I disagreed with Folsom's interpretation. The book is very well written and has a passion that is too rare in historical works. *Empire Builders* is an effective brief for the idea that the role of government in the economy should be limited.

William H. Mulligan, Jr.
Associate Professor of History, Murray State University
Former Director, Clarke Historical Library, Central Michigan University

With the grace of a master storyteller, Burt Folsom captures the spirit of such diverse figures as John Jacob Astor, Herbert Dow, Will Kellogg, and Henry Ford, affirming their efforts to forge a free and humane economy. Folsom's volume is a tribute not only to the general benefits of a free enterprise system, but also to Michigan's historical emphasis on limited government intervention into private commerce—a policy that has fostered and liberated the creative spirit of enterprise for the benefit of the state, the country, and the world.

Annette Kirk
Editor, *University Bookman*

Dr. Folsom has linked together the history of the most important pioneering entrepreneurs in Michigan's first century into a story that clearly reveals how heroic and persistent individual efforts were largely responsible for making the state an industrial giant. The author reaffirms the principle that individual entrepreneurship alone often determines the fate of communites and even states.

Jeremy W. Kilar
Professor of History, Delta College
Author of *Michigan's Lumbertowns, Saginaw's Changeable Past,* and *Bay City Logbook*

Empire Builders

How Michigan Entrepreneurs Helped Make America Great

BURTON W. FOLSOM, JR.

RHODES & EASTON
TRAVERSE CITY, MICHIGAN

Published by RHODES & EASTON
121 E. Front Street, 4th Floor, Traverse City, Michigan 49684
To order additional copies, please call: (800) 706-4636.

Publisher's Cataloging-in-Publication Data
Folsom, Burton W., Jr.
    Empire builders: how Michigan entrepreneurs helped make America great /
    Burton W. Folsom, Jr.; foreword by Governor John Engler. – Traverse City,
    MI: Rhodes & Easton, 1998.
        p. ill. cm.
    Includes index.
    ISBN 1-890394-06-8
    ISBN 1-890394-07-6 (paperback)
    1. Michigan—history. 2. Michigan—Biography. I. Title.
F566 .F65   1998   97-69249
977.4   dc—21   CIP

PROJECT COORDINATION BY JENKINS GROUP, INC.

02 01 00 99 ◆ 5 4 3 2 1

To
Anita Folsom,
Adam Folsom,
and
Burton W. Folsom, Sr.

MACKINAC CENTER
FOR PUBLIC POLICY

About the Mackinac Center for Public Policy

Empire Builders was published in cooperation with the Mackinac Center for Public Policy, a nonpartisan research and educational organization devoted to improving the quality of life for all Michigan citizens by promoting sound solutions to state and local policy questions. The Mackinac Center assists policy makers, scholars, business people, the media, and the public by providing objective analyses of Michigan issues. The goal of all Center reports, commentaries, and educational programs is to equip Michigan citizens and other decision makers to better evaluate policy options. The Mackinac Center for Public Policy is broadening the debate on issues that has for many years been dominated by the belief that government intervention should be the standard solution. Center publications and programs, in contrast, offer an integrated and comprehensive approach that considers:

All Institutions. The Center examines the important role of voluntary associations, businesses, communities, and families, as well as government.

All People. Mackinac Center research recognizes the diversity of Michigan citizens and treats them as individuals with unique backgrounds, circumstances, and goals.

All Disciplines. Mackinac Center research incorporates the best understanding of economics, science, law, psychology, history, and morality, moving beyond mechanical cost/benefit analysis.

All Times. Mackinac Center research evaluates long-term consequences, not simply the short-term impact.

Committed to independence, the Mackinac Center for Public Policy neither seeks nor accepts any government funding. It enjoys the support of foundations, individuals, and businesses who share a concern for Michigan's future and recognize the important role of sound ideas. The Center is a nonprofit, tax-exempt organization under Section 501 (c)(3) of the Internal Revenue Code. For more information on programs and publications of the Mackinac Center for Public Policy, please contact:

Mackinac Center for Public Policy
140 West Main • Midland, Michigan 48640
(517) 631-0900 • (517) 631-0964 fax
http://www.mackinac.org • mcpp@mackinac.org

Contents

Foreword

ICHIGAN IS FAMOUS NOT JUST FOR ITS LAKES, FORESTS, AND WINters, but for its remarkable entrepreneurs—people like the Fords, Durants, Kelloggs, and Dows—who transformed our state from a rustic wilderness into the industrial heart of North America.

It's hard for most Americans to go through a day without using a product developed by this amazing group of empire builders. If you eat cornflakes for breakfast, if you wrap your lunch with Saran Wrap, or if you drive a Chevy or a Ford, then you are using a product that originated in Michigan.

John Jacob Astor started Michigan's prominence by making fur hats from the beaver on and around Mackinac Island. After statehood, Henry Crapo came along and transformed the pine trees of eastern Michigan into houses built throughout the country. By the early 1900s, Fords were coming from Dearborn, Buicks and Chevys from Flint, All Bran and Rice Krispies from Battle Creek, and bleaches and dyes from Midland.

Dr. Folsom uses the metaphor "empire builder" to capture the global vision of Michigan's entrepreneurs. But these empires were built on service. As Folsom and others have noted, biblical wisdom was an ingredient to the success of these empire builders. "Give and it shall be given unto you," is a key principle in economic life. Michigan's entrepreneurs delayed the gratification of their own wants to satisfy the wants of others. They had faith that in free and open competition they could make products that would meet the needs of millions. Billy Durant, the founder of General Motors, remarked, "If I controlled the motor car business, the public would very likely get what I cared to build. With open competition, as we now have it, the people will get what they want. If I do not supply it, my competitors will."

What people wanted in the early 1900s was a reliable and affordable car that could take them where they wanted to go. In their day, Durant and Ford, with their Buicks and Model Ts, satisfied these wants better than any other two people in the world. Not only did they give the public the cheapest manufactured product in the world, the wages they paid made their workers the envy of industry everywhere. Also, as Ford helped to show, capitalism knew neither color nor caste. Whether a person was black or white, a recent immigrant or descendent of the original settlers, he could find a job with Ford Motor Company. No wonder millions of Americans flocked to Michigan. From 1900 to 1920, Flint alone soared from 13,000 to 91,000; Detroit skyrocketed from 286,000 to almost 1,000,000 people.

Michigan's empire builders were hardly an aristocracy or a titled elite. John Jacob Astor, the son of a butcher, immigrated to America as a young man. Billy Durant, a high school dropout, came to Flint with his mother after they were deserted by his alcoholic father. Will Kellogg, a bookkeeper for his brother, did not strike out on his own until he was 46 years old. Henry Ford grew up on a farm near Detroit. Herbert Dow's father was a humble mechanic. What they had in common was their willingness to risk their time, their savings, and their energy to develop "a better idea."

There is a lesson in the Michigan story for those of us in political life. Sometimes, the best thing government can do is to protect property and contracts, move out of the way, and let the entrepreneurs take risks. History shows that Michigan learned that lesson the hard way.

Stevens T. Mason, our first governor, wanted the state, not our entrepreneurs, to build Michigan's first railroads and canals. When the state entered the railroad business, the result was lobbying, bribery, and cost overruns. Finally, under Governor Alpheus Felch, we sold the railroads to private owners and they completed the building—with greater speed and better materials.

As a result of this experience, we amended our state constitution in 1850 to prevent such government interference in the future. Our liberties, however, were once again threatened by special interests. In the late 1860s, Governor Henry Crapo heroically, and almost on his death bed, vetoed bill after bill that would have allowed cities and towns to use local taxpayer dollars to subsidize more railroads.

The period from the ratification of the Constitution of 1850 to the Great Depression was the era of the empire builders in Michigan history. During these years, Michigan rose to prominence in the industrial history of the world. Those who liked Dr. Folsom's earlier book, *The Myth of the Robber Barons*, will appreciate this sequel. I strongly recommend this new book as a readable and fascinating history of a remarkable group of entrepreneurs who first changed Michigan, and then changed the world.

Governor John Engler
Lansing, Michigan

Acknowledgments

THE RISE OF MICHIGAN FROM A SWAMPLAND TO THE AUTO CAPITAL of the world is a story worth telling. In fact, if we understand the Michigan story we understand a crucial part of how America became great. Michigan's industrial triumph did two things. First, it helped elevate the U. S. to its position as the major economic power in the world by the early 1920s. Second, it shifted much economic power within the U.S. from the East to the Midwest.

A key ingredient in Michigan's success was the presence of some of the greatest entrepreneurs in U. S. history. John Jacob Astor, the wealthiest man in America, made the Michigan Territory the base for his American Fur Company in the early 1800s. Later in the century, Henry Ford, William Durant, Herbert Dow, and Will Kellogg all had their creative starts in Michigan's open economic environment. What they did and how they did it is the heart of this book.

Many people have helped make this book possible. Special thanks go to William Mulligan, professor of history and former director of the Clarke Library at Central Michigan University. He read and critiqued this manuscript and shared with me his wide knowledge of Michigan history.

I had help on each chapter from experts in their fields. I thank John Haeger, John Jacob Astor's best biographer, for making suggestions on my Astor chapter. The Stevens T. Mason chapter benefited from encouragement from Leroy Barnett, an authority on Michigan's early railroads. Jeremy Kilar, an expert on Michigan's lumber industry, critiqued this entire book, and especially my chapters on lumber and autos. E. N. Brandt, Herbert Dow's biographer, and Ted Doan, former CEO at The Dow Chemical Company, were indispensible in helping me understand Herbert Dow and the early chemical industry. They both read my Dow chapter and saved me from many errors, large and small. Anthony Hebron, the archivist at the Kellogg Company, has improved my Kellogg chapter, and so has Joel Orosz.

Several librarians helped make my research productive. The staffs at the Bentley Library at the University of Michigan, the Clarke and Park Libraries at Central Michigan University, and the Michigan State Archives in Lansing were helpful. So was Kathy Thomas at the Post Street Archives in Midland and Bill Holleran at the General Motors Institute Alumni Historical Library.

Special thanks also to Tim Nash, academic dean at Northwood University, and to my students in economic history at Northwood University, who read this book as a class project and helped me rethink several parts of it.

My colleagues at the Mackinac Center for Public Policy have given me peace and help, whichever I have happened to need. Lawrence Reed wanted me to do this book even before I joined the Center. He has guided it from the start and has read each chapter carefully. Joseph Overton, Joseph Lehman, and Michael LaFaive also read this book and made encouraging suggestions. Kendra Shrode has listened patiently when I have lectured around the state on Michigan entrepreneurs. Matthew Wilczek and Peter Leeson double-checked foot-notes for me; LeAnn Harlow made many copies of the chapters; and Jeffrey Tucker bailed me out whenever my computer decided to be ornery. Amy Kellogg, our "comma queen," has been a valuable proof-reader. James Kostrava, in a brainstorming session one day, suggested the title for the book. For my Ford chapter, Robert Hunter and William Maze discussed the Wagner Act and collective bargaining with me. Nancy Hinchcliff, Catherine Martin, Todd Crelly, and Joi Henton cheered me up on days when I struggled with writing.

David Littmann, William B. Allen, Annette Kirk, Tom Bray, George Roche, Gleaves Whitney, and John Engler are among the finest intel-lects in the state of Michigan. Their individual endorsements of this book have been a strong encouragement and a delightful surprise. At Rhodes & Easton, Mark Dressler, Anne Stanton, and Sydney McManus have been supportive and helpful.

My wife, Anita, has read each chapter and has listened to me prat-tle on about entrepreneurs when I should have been mowing the lawn. My son Adam, however, has been mowing the lawn and showing a flair for business. My father, the original Burt Folsom, has always believed in me, and has thereby shown me the importance of risk and faith in life.

Introduction

"I SHALL BEGIN WITH OUR ANCESTORS," PERICLES SAID OVER 2,400 years ago in his Funeral Oration. "And if our remote ancestors deserve praise, much more do our own fathers, who added to their inheritance the empire which we now possess, and spared no pains to be able to leave their acquisitions to us of the present generation."[1]

The Greeks, like most ancient civilizations, had a keen sense of their history. The Hebrews did, too. The Old Testament rings with prophets' warnings to the Hebrews not to forget the great triumphs Jehovah had given them. They carried the ark of the covenant with them, they celebrated the Passover, and they put stones in the middle of the Jordan River—all to remind them what Jehovah had done for them.

The American civilization, which has been strongly influenced by both the Greeks and Hebrews, needs to better imitate their love of the past and their celebration of what brought them to greatness. In the case of the U. S., we can pinpoint a time when it rose to world dominance—the late 1800s and early 1900s. We can pinpoint a group of entrepreneurs who built economic empires that caused the balance of power in the world to shift from Europe to the United States.

Finally, we can pinpoint a strong Judaeo-Christian culture with limited government and much individual liberty in which this triumph took place. This convergence of a time period, a group of heroes, and a spirit of the age is a story worth telling.

In ancient days, heroes and their victories were celebrated and remembered in epic poems, psalms, and speeches. Future generations, therefore, had role models to admire, stories to repeat, and a heritage to preserve. When we tell the story of how the U. S. became a world power, we also have triumphant heroes, dramatic stories, and a useful heritage to study and learn.

One of the most exciting batch of stories comes out of Michigan—an underdog state long dismissed as a frozen wasteland. From the time Michigan entered the union in 1837, the governor and the legislators wanted to make the state an economic powerhouse. Their first effort was to enlist massive government aid in building railroads and canals throughout Michigan.

When this experiment with state control failed, they tried free enterprise and individual liberty. They sold the railroads to private owners and, when that succeeded, they wrote a new constitution that opened Michigan to entrepreneurs and barred the state from intruding on private enterprise. Michigan's future would be in the hands of its entrepreneurs.

How well did this experiment work? Let's look at some examples. In 1883, a young physician named William was troubled by problems he had with pills that would not dissolve in the stomachs of his patients. William set aside his mornings—prime earning hours for physicians—and went up to the small attic of his house in Hastings, Michigan, where he did experiment after experiment to make better pills. He rejected the standard method of making pills from paste; instead he created them from "starter particles." He added powdered drugs and moistening agents to these particles while he rotated them in a revolving pan. The result was a pill that held its contents, but was soft enough to dissolve easily when swallowed.

In 1885, William—Dr. William E. Upjohn—patented his "friable pill," as he called it, and started the Upjohn Pill and Granule Company in a small brick building in nearby Kalamazoo. His first price list included 186 pill formulas—quinine pills, iron pills, anti-constipation pills, and many others. Over the next six years, Upjohn sold millions of pills and generated the capital needed to enter the pharmaceutical market. In the next forty years, whether making laxatives or vitamin D capsules, Dr. Upjohn marketed a superior product that sold widely throughout the United States and even the world.[2]

One thing to note about Dr. Upjohn is that his business did not rely on any natural resources found in Michigan. He could have done his experiments and started his company outside of Michigan. He stayed in Michigan, though, because the economic system there triggered his entrepreneurial energy and allowed him to keep the profits he made. Let's look at another example that parallels the Upjohn story.

One Sunday evening in 1927 in the town of Fremont, Michigan, a young married man named Dan waited impatiently for his wife Dorothy to feed their daughter, who was seven months old. They had a social engagement that evening and Dan was ready to go. He paced back and forth, looking at his watch and waiting. Dorothy, meanwhile, was tediously straining vegetables into a bowl, piece by piece by tiny piece. Soon fidgety Dan stomped into the kitchen, pleading with his wife to hurry up. That's when Dorothy decided to teach him a lesson. "To press the point," Dorothy later recalled, "I dumped a whole container of peas into a strainer and bowl, placed them in Dan's lap, and asked him to see how he'd like to do that three times a day, seven days a week."[3]

Dan got the message. The next day, when he went to work in his family-owned cannery, he had an idea for something new to put in the cans: baby food, already strained and ready to serve. During the next year, Dan Gerber would establish the baby food market and then dominate it for decades. He test marketed strained carrots, peas, prunes, and spinach on babies right there in Fremont, Michigan. Then he persuaded grocery stores around the country to carry his canned baby food. During his first year, mothers all over the country chose to save time and energy more than their cash; they bought 590,000 cans of Gerber's baby food at 15 cents per can. Dorothy Gerber, now liberated from straining vegetables, started a newspaper column, "Bringing Up Baby," in which she answered thousands of questions about feeding and raising children.

Gerber's baby food, like Upjohn's pills, did not need Michigan's resources to flourish. But they both needed Michigan's entrepreneurial spirit and freedom from heavy taxation and stifling regulation. In the late 1800s and early 1900s, of course, the whole United States had a small federal government, no income tax, and strong constitutional support for free enterprise. Most states also encouraged individual freedom and limited government. Michigan especially, through its liberating state constitution, went out of the way to limit its government and stake the state's future on what its entrepreneurs could accomplish.

Even Thomas Edison had his start in Michigan. In 1854, at age 7, Edison moved from Ohio to Port Huron, Michigan, where his father started a feed and grain business. At age 12, young Edison sold newspapers and peanuts on the train from Port Huron to Detroit. During his layovers in Detroit, Edison discovered the science books in the Detroit Public Library and read them with keen interest. He even set up a laboratory in the corner of the train's baggage car.

A turning point in Edison's life came in 1862 while he was waiting for a train in Mt. Clemens. A small boy, the son of the station agent, was playing in the gravel between the tracks when a freight car came rumbling down the line toward him. Edison rushed toward the boy, grabbed him, and jumped off the tracks just in time to save them both. The grateful station agent thanked Edison and taught him all about the telegraph business and how to use Morse code. Soon Edison was making his living as a telegraph operator. At age 22, after he had left Michigan, he sold an improved type of telegraph equipment, his first marketable invention, for $40,000—enough to start Edison on a life as a full-time inventor.[4]

Some of this creativity in Michigan was minor, such as Fred Sanders inventing the ice cream soda in 1875, or James Vernor serving the world's first carbonated soft drink in 1866 (Vernor's ginger ale). Other entrepreneurs made major breakthroughs. Eber Ward became a multimillionaire through his Eureka Iron and Steel Company in Detroit. In 1864, the Eureka firm became the first American enterprise to make steel through the new Bessemer process. In the 1920s, the Perrigo Company in Allegan, Michigan, became a major innovator in pharmaceuticals by creating the "private label" concept. They imprinted the names of individual stores on the aspirin, epsom salts, and toothpaste they sold.[5]

Even black Americans, who were subject to much discrimination, had opportunities in Michigan. A good example is the great inventor, Elijah McCoy. McCoy was born in 1843 in Canada, where his parents had fled from Kentucky to escape slavery. After the Civil War had ended, and blacks were legally free, McCoy came back to the U. S. to enjoy this freedom. He settled in Ypsilanti, Michigan, where he began work for the Michigan Central Railroad as a locomotive fireman.[6]

McCoy immediately applied his skills to a major problem: the dangerous overheating of locomotives. Trains had to stop regularly to oil engine parts to reduce friction. If trains stopped infrequently, the overheating could damage parts or start fires. If they stopped too often, freight and passengers would be delayed. McCoy invented a lubricating cup that oiled engine parts as the train was moving. He secured a patent for it in 1872 and steadily improved it over time.

Others tried to imitate McCoy's invention, but he kept ahead of them with his superior engineering skills. His standard of quality was so high that to separate his lubricating cup from cheaper imitations it became known as "the real McCoy," which many believe to be the origin of the famous phrase.

McCoy showed remarkable creative energy during the next fifty years. He received 51 more patents for inventions ranging from a forerunner of the ironing board to a special cup for administering medicine. Not even old age dimmed his creative light. When he was 77, he patented an improved airbrake lubricator; when he was 80, he patented a vehicle wheel tire. He founded the Elijah McCoy Manufacturing Company in Detroit in 1920 to make and sell his inventions.

McCoy was not an isolated example of black entrepreneurship. In 1887, Fred Pelham was president of his class at the University of Michigan. From there he became assistant civil engineer with the Michigan Central Railroad. His innovations in structure and design included the "skew arch" bridge type; and some of the twenty bridges he built still stand in Michigan today.[7] The obstacles facing minority entrepreneurs were substantial, but many did overcome them and used their freedom to excel in Michigan's economic life.

Why, then, did so much of the building of the American empire take place in Michigan? To find out we need to see why Michigan chose free enterprise over government direction. Then we need to study what Michigan's risk-takers accomplished. Six chapters in this book tell the stories of seven key men—six entrepreneurs and a politician—who forged Michigan's industrial growth. They include John Jacob Astor, who centered his fur trading in the Michigan Territory in the early 1800s. After statehood, Henry Crapo helped Michigan become the top lumber-producing state in the union. Lumbering enabled entrepreneurs in Michigan to diversify into carriages. The next step was autos, and Henry Ford and William Durant made their state the world center for one of the greatest industries of the 20th century. Michigan was also the place where Herbert Dow helped break forever the European monopolies in chemicals; and where Will Kellogg made cornflakes and changed breakfast habits throughout the Western world.

None of these men started life in luxury, but all became remarkably successful. Two of them even became the wealthiest men in America; two others became governors of Michigan. Some were well-educated; others were barely literate. Some had bland personalities; others were flamboyant and eccentric almost to the point of lunacy. One man, John Jacob Astor, had little permanent effect on Michigan; another, Stevens T. Mason, is the politician whose state-financed railroad scheme backfired and led to more free enterprise later. The others took hold of the opportunities Michigan deliberately created and changed dramatically the world they were born into.

The ancient Greeks would have been fascinated by Michigan's empire builders. William Durant and Stevens T. Mason were tragic figures, whose rise to greatness carried within it the seeds of later destruction. Herbert Dow, whom the Germans targeted for annihilation, launched a surprise attack and broke the German monopolies in bromine and indigo. The ancient Hebrews might have seen in Henry Ford and Will Kellogg the fulfillment of biblical scriptures: "Give and it shall be given unto you," Jesus said, and "If anyone wants to be first he must be the very last, and the servant of all."[8] Henry Ford gave the world a cheap reliable car and the world gave him over one billion dollars. Will Kellogg spent decades in the wilderness, the servant of his domineering brother. With perseverance and hard work he invented and perfected flaked cereals and finished life strong, full of years, and a benefactor for millions of Americans.

John Jacob Astor, a real-life Horatio Alger, dominated the U.S. fur trade despite some attempts by the U.S government to legislate him out of business.

1

John Jacob Astor and the Fur Trade:
Testing the Role of Government

ONE HUNDRED YEARS AGO THE BEST-SELLING NOVELS IN AMERICA were written by Horatio Alger. His storyline is a familiar one. An immigrant comes to America seeking his fortune. He begins by doing menial tasks and then, by pluck and luck, climbs the ladder of success. He finds a good product to sell and soon starts his own business. He competes head to head with other companies, led by educated men from fine families. He confronts obstacles and challenges a swindler in the marketplace. In the end, the skill, the pluck, and the drive of the immigrant help him triumph over all adversity.[1]

Even before Horatio Alger began writing these types of novels, the United States had its own real life Horatio Alger story, and much of it was lived out in Michigan. The hero was John Jacob Astor, a multimillionaire fur trader and the first U. S. entrepreneur to challenge a government-run business.

To understand Astor, we need to start with the fur trade. The buying and selling of furs was a major industry in America throughout its early history. The key animal in the fur trade was the beaver, whose pelt made hats that were in style all over Europe in the 1700s. The fur trade was a worldwide enterprise. It linked fashionable women in Paris to New York exporters, to frontier traders, to Indian trappers. The pelts of beavers, muskrats, otters, and minks went one way and kettles, blankets, axes, and muskets went the other.[2]

At first, fur trading in the U. S. followed established patterns. The French and British had traded with the Indians for more than a century and the Americans simply picked up where they left off. Trapping methods, river routes, and trading posts were all in place.[3]

The man who confounded the normal development of private enterprise in furs was none other than President George Washington. Washington grew up in an era of mercantilism: Governments would freely grant monopolies to gain certain political and economic advantages.

Adam Smith, of course, challenged this kind of thinking in 1776 in *The Wealth of Nations*, but ideas take time to percolate. Washington viewed the British fur traders in the Michigan area, then the Northwest Territory, as a menace to America's future. They might stir up the Indians, win their loyalties, and thwart U. S. expansion into its Northwest Territory.[4]

Private American traders, Washington argued, were too few to compete with the larger, more experienced British. The U. S. government itself was needed to build large trading posts, oust the British, "bring in a small profit, . . . and fix them [the Indians] strongly in our Interest." The Indians especially needed to see evidence of American strength, so Washington recommended that the government build and operate a series of fur factories throughout the American South and Northwest. With Washington's support, Congress appropriated $50,000 for the new factories in 1795 and raised it steadily in later years to $300,000. [5] Such a subsidy was a large expense for a new nation, and one that tested government's ability to be an entrepreneur.

Here is how the factory system worked. The government created a bureaucracy—the Office of Indian Affairs—to conduct the fur trade. It used the $300,000 from Congress to set up trading posts (usually near military forts), stock them with goods, and pay agents to buy, store, and transfer furs from the trading post to Washington, D. C., where they would be sold at auction. Once the factories were funded, they were supposed to be self-supporting, and perhaps, as Washington said, "bring in a small profit." Agents in the factories would use the first batch of goods to buy furs; then when the furs were sold, the agents could buy more goods and repeat the cycle.[6]

Almost from the start, however, the factory system struggled. Well into the 1800s, the British companies were trading actively throughout the Great Lakes area. So were private American traders. The factories were so poorly run that many Indians held them in contempt and refused to trade there. In 1816, President Monroe appointed Thomas McKenney, a Washington merchant, to take charge of the Office of Indian Affairs and help the factories expand their business.[7]

Tall, with fiery red hair and a hook nose, McKenney worked hard and took his job seriously. He wrote long letters to Indians, invited them to Washington, and tried to expand his staff so he could deal with them more directly. Indians needed to be assimilated into American life, McKenney argued. Schools and farms, not trapping and hunting, were McKenney's vision for future Indian life. An active government, McKenney believed, was the best means to trade with the Indians and help them assimilate into American culture.[8]

As chief officer of the government fur trade, McKenney put his stamp on the business in many ways. First, he tried to slash costs by limiting credit and gifts—some called them bribes—to the Indians. Giving gifts had long been a custom in the fur trade, and many Indians requested credit for supplies for trapping. Both trends, to McKenney, were expensive and risky and he stopped them when he could.

Second, McKenney tried to "buy American" for the factories when possible. Indians, for example, needed muskets. McKenney responded by rejecting English imports and giving large contracts to Henry Deringer, which helped establish him as a major weapons producer.

Third, McKenney so much wanted Indians to become farmers that he stocked the factories with hoes, plows, and other farm equipment. It was part of his campaign to "amend the heads and hearts of the Indians." He urged agents at the factories to have gardens outside their walls to show the Indians what they could grow if they would just exchange their pelts for plows.[9]

McKenney's ideas were a disaster. Indians wanted gifts, needed credit, and shunned plows. But since McKenney was funded regularly each year by government, regardless of his volume of trade, he had no incentive to change his tactics.[10] Private traders, however, had to please Indians or go broke. As private traders grew in numbers and wealth in the early 1800s, one of them, John Jacob Astor, grew so rich he surpassed the government factories in capital, influence, and volume of business.

Astor, the son of a German butcher, came to the U. S. in 1784 at age 20 to join his brother in selling violins and flutes. Soon, however, he changed his tune. He became fascinated with the fur trade and studied it day and night. He learned prices, markets, and trade routes for all kinds of pelts. The fur territory of New York and Montreal became Astor's domain of trade. He bought and sold cautiously at first, then with more confidence as the profits rolled in.[11]

He was an odd man to be such a risk-taker. He was quiet, almost secretive, in his business dealings. Astor had a keen mind for enterprise, but he spent years at a time out of the United States, estranged from his wife and fighting bouts of depression. He was both decisive

Courtesy of the Clarke Historical Library

An American Fur Company warehouse (c. 1903) that housed furs in the early 1800s. The furs were shipped all over the world.

and patient. He had a vision of how America would grow, how the fur trade fit into that growth, and how to market furs around the world. With commanding vision and masterful detail he could profitably buy furs in Michigan, pack them on a boat to New York, ship them to China, and bring tea back home.[12]

Astor separated himself from others through his foresight and perseverance. If the matrons of France wanted beaver hats and otter coats, and if these these animals roamed the forests of New York, that was all most traders cared to know.

Astor, however, thought more of world trade. Europeans liked to fight each other; wars disrupted markets. Why not expand and sell furs to the Chinese—not for fashion, but for warmth in their unheated houses? Besides, he could bring the tea back from China and profit at both ends.[13]

The large market of the Far East prompted Astor to turn his sights west to Michigan. New York and the Atlantic coast were depleted of furs by the early 1800s. The Great Lakes area—especially the Michigan Territory—then became the heart of the fur trade and pumped out

Astor traded the best supplies he could find for the Indians at a reasonable rate of exchange. His Michigan trading posts were similar to the one pictured above, at Fond du Lac, Wisconsin.

thousands of skins for coats and rugs all over the world. Astor founded the American Fur Company in 1808 and made his move to challenge the government factories.[14]

Under Astor, the American Fur Company resembled a modern corporation with specialists, division of labor, and vertical integration. He ran the company from his headquarters in New York. Mackinac Island, in the Michigan Territory, was the center of the actual trading, where most furs were bought, packed on boats, and sent over to the east coast. Astor's agents dotted the rivers throughout the Northwest and they had log cabins well-stocked with goods. They supplied the company's fur traders, who would live with the different Indian tribes and supply them with goods and credit as needed.[15]

In conducting business this way, Astor differed from McKenney and the government factories. McKenney and his predecessors just built trading posts, stocked them with goods, and expected the Indians to come there to trade. Many Indians, however, lived hundreds of miles from a factory and had no supplies to trap with. Even if McKenney had given credit easily, and had known whom to trust, the Indians would have been hampered by distances. Under Astor's system, the fur traders lived with the Indians, learned whom to trust, and bought and sold on the spot. If an Ottawa brave capsized his canoe and lost his musket and powder, he could get replacements from Astor's local trader and avoid the ninety-mile walk through swirling snow to see if the government agent in Detroit would give him replacements on credit.[16]

Astor built on this advantage by trading the best supplies he could find at reasonable rates of exchange. Indians wanted guns and blankets, for example, and Astor supplied them at low costs. The best blankets he could find were British-made blue-striped blankets, and Astor bought them at 15 percent less than McKenney paid for lower quality blankets made in America. Astor bought British Tower muskets, the best on the market, for about $10 each, but McKenney paid $12.50 apiece for Henry Deringer's muskets made in Philadelphia.[17]

One reason Astor succeeded was that he accepted the Indians as they were, not as he wanted them to be. If they desired axes, kettles, and muskets, he found the best available and sold them at competitive prices. He respected Indians as shrewd traders and knew he had to have the best goods to get the most business. McKenney, as we have seen, squandered government resources on hoes and plows that went unsold. He also bought jew's harps by the gross, and they sat on the shelves gathering dust. One time McKenney splurged and bought a Chinese Mandarin dress, which he sent to the Osage factory along with a note admitting it would be hard to sell.[18]

McKenney was frustrated with Indian culture and wanted to change it. He refused to sell liquor in government factories and urged Indians to be sober, virtuous, and industrious. "The same devotion to the chase, and those irregular habits which have characterized the sons of our forests yet predominate," he lamented.[19]

Liquor was also an item Astor preferred not to supply, even though he knew many Indians wanted it. Not that Astor was a moralist; he was a realist. Drunken trappers gathered no pelts, he discovered. If the factories had been his only competition he probably wouldn't have traded liquor at all. But the traders with Britain's Hudson's Bay Company carried so much liquor they could almost have created another Great Lake with it. Astor thus believed that for him to be competitive he needed to have some liquor available for trade.

Ramsay Crooks, Astor's chief administrator, stated company policy this way: "If the Government permit[s] the sale of this pernicious liquid we can have no hesitation in availing ourselves of the privilege, though we are convinced its total prohibition would benefit both the country at large and the natives who are its victims."[20]

Trade was not the only area where Astor outmaneuvered the government factories. The motivating of men was another. Astor used a merit system to reward his top producers. "As with skins," he said, "for good men we cannot pay too dear & indifferent ones are at any price too dear." Astor paid his chief managers good salaries plus a share of the profits. This guaranteed attention to detail, which Astor needed to stay on top. McKenney and his staff, by contrast, received a standard salary from Congress with no bonuses given in profitable years or cuts given when trade fell. If McKenney had been on a merit system, he might have been less moved to stock his factories with plows, jew's harps, and Chinese dresses.[21]

One final area of Astor's genius was his marketing savvy. He sold his furs at auctions all over the world. If he didn't get the prices he wanted in New York, he sent furs to auctions in Montreal, London, Hamburg, St. Petersburg, and Canton. He studied the bidding, searched for trends, and moved quickly when prices changed. Deerskins, Astor once predicted, would go up in price in Hamburg; muskrat would sell higher in St. Petersburg, Philadelphia, and Canton. He acted accordingly and reaped strong profits in each of these cities.

Another Astor strategy was this: If he sensed an upward trend in the price of raccoon skins he would alert his agents to collect all they could get. If demand slowed and prices dropped, Astor withdrew his raccoon skins and stored them in New York, Paris, or Canton until prices rose.[22]

McKenney, by contrast, lacked sophistication. He had those furs collected in his factories sent to Washington. Then he sold them at auction in nearby Georgetown for whatever price they would bring. He didn't sell in different cities, nor did he withhold any from the market in bad years. But then again he had no incentive to study prices, trends, and foreign markets because his salary was constant whether or not he made profits. In any case, even if he had developed insights into markets, Congress might not have approved the risks and costs of storing beaver pelts during depressions, or overcollecting deerskins to send to Hamburg.[23]

Sometime after 1808, John Jacob Astor surpassed the government factories and emerged as the leading exporter of furs in the U. S. He widened his lead after the War of 1812. By the 1820s, his American Fur Company employed over 750 men, not counting the Indians, and collected annual fur harvests of about $500,000, which made it one of the largest companies in America.

Many independents also popped up to trade furs. For example, William Ashley in St. Louis, Menard and Valle in Illinois, and the Rocky Mountain Fur Company out west all traded furs aggressively. The government system of expecting Indians to come to the factories to trade was proving to be outmoded.[24]

McKenney nervously watched the government's share of the fur trade decline year by year. "Why do the factories lose money?" Congress asked when McKenney came before them each year to renew his subsidy. He was embarrassed by Astor's dominance and perplexed at what to do about it. At one point, he urged his agents, or "factors" as they were called, to stir up Indians against private traders. "[A]ll correct means that may be taken to expel those traders," McKenney wrote, would be "of service to humanity and justice."

What these "correct means" were became clearer when he told his factor to impress the Osages "with the belief that such is the design of those traders . . . that [the Indians] must get rid of them; & hope not to be accountable for their own efforts to drive them out." To another factor, he wrote, "I should judge, with your long acquaintance with the Indian tempers, you might upon the most humane and honourable grounds, turn their prejudices against these their enemies [i.e., private traders]."[25]

When sabotage failed, McKenney briefly copied Astor's technique of directly trading with the Indians. He sent out "subtraders," people who took government goods from the factories directly to the Indians. He took this step very reluctantly. "It will be necessary for you to use extreme caution in trusting out goods to traders," McKenney wrote one of his factors. "Boats may get upset . . . and even if . . . they should escape being drowned, the tommahawk [sic] may put them to rest—and relieve you from the trouble of counting their returns." Nonetheless, he used subtraders in Green Bay and Chicago and reported "an [i]ncrease of factory business. . . ." But it didn't last. Astor and the private traders were too shrewd and aggressive for McKenney and they soon recaptured lost markets.[26]

By 1818, McKenney had reached a dramatic conclusion: The best way to beat Astor was to influence Congress to ban the private fur traders. If this could be done, McKenney could monopolize the fur trade, sell the Indians what he wanted them to have, and pursue his dream of amending their heads and hearts. McKenney's chief ally in the House of Representatives was Henry Southard, chairman of the House Committee on Indian Affairs. In a letter to Southard, McKenney argued vigorously for a government monopoly. "I know of no check that could be devised having such a powerful influence as that which this sort of dependence would impose on the Indians," McKenney wrote Southard. "Armies themselves would not be so effectual in regulating the native Inhabitants as would a state of dependence on the Government for their commercial intercourse." Sure, McKenney admitted, a monopoly "embraces the idea of compulsion." But "the power over the Indians is covetted [sic] only for their good—and also to prevent them from doing harm."[27]

To John C. Calhoun, secretary of war and later vice president, McKenney wrote that the factory system "has its foundation in benevolence and reform." The private traders, by contrast, wanted only profits. They didn't care about reforming the Indian, McKenney argued, and they even sold him liquor. Calhoun liked McKenney and seems to have been persuaded if not for a monopoly at least for greater government control. "The trade should," Calhoun wrote, "as far as practicable, be put effectually under the control of the Government, in order that . . . [the Indians] may be protected against the fraud and the violence to which their ignorance and weakness would, without such protection, expose them."[28]

Even with friends in high places, however, McKenney couldn't muster the support in Congress to ban private fur trading. He therefore presented two backup plans. First, the government should increase his subsidy from $300,000 to $500,000. That way he could build eight new factories west of the Mississippi River, which would increase his trade with distant Indians, bring American culture to them, and thereby "serve the great object of humanity."[29]

Second, McKenney wanted to increase the license fees for his competitors. If he couldn't ban private fur traders by law, perhaps he could raise their costs of doing business, and thereby improve the competitive position of the factories. Under existing law, anyone who posted a $1,000 bond could buy a $5 license from an Indian agent and trade for two years. McKenney wanted to increase the license fee to $10,000. He argued that hordes of unlicensed traders roamed the West buying furs and selling whiskey. A higher license fee and stiffer penalties, McKenney argued, would slash the number of traders and make them easier to regulate and supervise.[30]

Astor was appalled at McKenney's schemes. Astor could view himself as the top fur trader in the country, a man popular with Indians because he gave them what they wanted, where they wanted it, and when they wanted it. He catered to Indians as consumers and gave them some of the best prices available for axes, kettles, and blankets. McKenney, by contrast, expected Indians to march hundreds of miles to factories to trade for plows they didn't want or muskets they did want, but not at McKenney's high prices. Then when the Indians wouldn't come he tried to ban his competitors, calling them profiteers and calling himself a humanitarian.[31]

Astor hated to play politics, but he believed he had to be politically shrewd to survive. He wrote to President Monroe and explained how the American Fur Company helped the U. S. economy. He sent Ramsay Crooks, his chief agent, to Washington to talk with congressmen, and even put some of them on his payroll. Other politicians came to Astor's aid. Governor Ninian Edwards of the Illinois Territory challenged Calhoun: "For my part, I have never been able to discover, and I defy any man to specify, a solitary public advantage that has resulted from it [the factory system] in this country." Governor Lewis Cass of the Michigan Territory told Calhoun that the government factories were "obnoxious and contemptible" to the Indians. "The Government," Cass said, "should never [c]ome into contact with them, but in cases where its [d]ignity, its strength or its liberality will inspire them with respect or fear."[32]

From 1816 to 1822, Congress heard from both sides and had frequent debates on the fur trade. The bill to ban private traders, Astor was pleased to learn, never made it out of the House Committee on Indian Affairs. Neither did the bill to increase McKenney's subsidy to $500,000.[33]

In 1820, however, the Senate passed a bill to force each trader to post a $10,000 bond for the right to trade. The government, through Calhoun and McKenney, would be in charge of issuing licenses and they had the right to turn down unsuitable applicants. When the bill went to the House, Astor's friends sprang into action. "What is this but giving to the Sec[retar]y at War power to create a Monopoly?" asked William Woodbridge, the Michigan Territory's delegate to Congress. "The plain English is that all our citizens are if possible to be excluded from the Indian trade . . . [and] the . . . Factory Gen[tleme]n are to take it all. . . ."[34]

Ramsay Crooks worked overtime in Washington exhorting House members to quash the new license bill. One of the weapons in his arsenal was an eight-page pamphlet he circulated to challenge McKenney's "perversion of facts." The pamphlet excoriated the factory system:

> It never drove a foreign trader from the country; it never ministered to the wants, or relieved the necessities of the Indians in the day of distress; and no instance can be adduced, of its ever composing the differences of contending tribes.[35]

The prospects of another government-licensing bureaucracy must have alarmed Astor. Four years earlier Congress had passed a law requiring all foreigners to be licensed to trade.

Before Astor's staff of traders was notified of that law, Major William Puthuff, the federal Indian agent at Mackinac Island, arrested them as they brought furs to his headquarters on the island. Puthuff used four boats to patrol the island and seized furs from all unlicensed traders—Americans and foreigners alike—throughout the summer in 1816.

He further harassed Astor by arbitrarily raising the license fees from $5 to $50. Astor finally protested to Calhoun, and Calhoun eventually fired Puthuff. The new licensing bill, like the old one, promised more bureaucrats and fewer traders in the American West.[36]

After a hard-fought debate on licensing, Astor won and the House refused to act on the Senate's bill. Crooks was ecstatic. "[H]ad Mr. Secretary Calhoun carried his point in getting the proposed law passed," he wrote Astor, "it is no longer concealed that his first step was to license so few traders that the factories were sure of reviving." Without more government help, McKenney was in trouble. His eight factories showed a drop in fur sales from $73,305 in 1816 to $28,482 in 1819. The next year, during the debate on the licensing bill, one of his factors told him that his trade had "almost [e]ntirely ceased."[37]

With McKenney weakened, Astor took the offensive and urged Congress to abolish the whole factory system. Step one for Astor was to help Congress to see how unpopular the factories were with Indians. Calhoun, McKenney's ally, unwittingly cooperated when, as secretary of war, he helped authorize Jedidiah Morse, a Congregational minister, to go into Indian country and report on the Indian trade. Astor and McKenney had made so many charges and countercharges that Calhoun wanted to get reliable independent information on the issue. He told Morse to "report such facts, as may come within your knowledge, as will go to show the state of the trade with them [the Indians], and the character of the traders, and will suggest such improvements in the present system of trade." Morse was considered a neutral observer and his first-hand report would be the most systematic investigation of the government factories ever done. [38]

Morse visited most of the government factories and interviewed the men who worked in them as well as the private traders nearby. He talked with many tribes of Indians about the fur trade, studied their habits, and recorded their views. He spent almost four months in travel—including 12 days in Detroit and 16 days on Mackinac Island—and even longer writing up his research.[39]

In his report he came down clearly against the factories. "In the first place," Morse wrote, "I have to observe that the Factory system . . . does not appear to me to be productive of any great advantage, either to the Indians themselves, or to the Government." This conclusion was devastating because it revealed that the factory system had failed to do what Washington had set it up to do—impress the Indians, gain their respect, and challenge the British in the Northwest Territory. Morse further wrote that "the Indians, who are good judges of the quality of the articles they want, are of the opinion that the Factor[y]'s goods are not so cheap, taking into consideration their quality, as those of private traders." Even John Johnson, the factor at Prairie du Chien, admitted he had received expensive goods from McKenney that were "inferior and unsuitable [in] quality for Indian trade."[40]

Morse was not completely pleased with private traders. They traded too much whiskey, he wrote, and they gave Indians too much on credit, which weakened their work ethic. But he couldn't deny their success or the "want of confidence in the Government . . . expressed by the Indians in my interviews with them." Abolishing the factories, Morse concluded, was

> decidedly the best course, the best adopted to raise and preserve the reputation of the Government in the estimation of Indians, and to secure for it their confidence and respect; the best fitted in all respects to accomplish the great object of imparting to them the blessings of civilization and Christianity.[41]

Armed with the Morse report, Astor's allies in Congress moved to abolish the factories in 1822. Thomas Hart Benton, the new senator from Missouri, had been a lawyer for Astor and knew the fur trade well. On the Senate floor he ridiculed McKenney's purchases, particularly the eight gross (1,152) jew's harps he had recently sent to the factories. What use, Benton asked, could Indians have for jew's harps? "I know!" he said sarcastically. "They are part of McKenney's schemes to amend the heads and hearts of the Indians, to improve their moral and intellectual faculties, and to draw them from the savage and hunter state, and induct them into the innocent pursuits of civilized life."[42]

Not surprisingly, Benton urged Congress to end the factory system. "[E]very public consideration," Benton argued, "requires it to be immediately abolished, the accounts of all concerned be settled up and closed, the capital be returned to the public treasury, the salaries of all officers be stopped, and its profit and loss be shown at the next session of Congress." Most Congressmen agreed. The Senate voted 17 to 11 to end the factories; the House soon followed; and on May 6, 1822, President Monroe signed Benton's bill.[43]

The closing of the factories was a story in itself. The merchandise inside them was to be collected and sold at auctions around the country. The money received would then be returned to the government to offset the $300,000 federal subsidy. Congress entrusted the treasury department, not McKenney, with closing the factories and holding the auctions. In doing their work, the officials in the treasury department were stunned at how unpopular the factory goods were. Lewis Cass, who had a batch sent to him in the Michigan Territory, was appalled at their poor quality. "These goods," Cass said, "were selected I presume, as the worst and most unsaleable in the factories, and certainly they well deserve this character. They are not fit for distribution. . . ." Others agreed. The auctions themselves, which became the true test of the market value of the articles in the factories, brought grim news. The government, on its $300,000 investment, received a return of only $56,038.15. As Senator Benton had said, "The factory system grew out of a national calamity, and has been one itself."[44]

Many congressmen were astounded at the waste of government

funds revealed by the auctions. If Astor could make millions of dollars trading furs, how could the government lose hundreds of thousands? Critics demanded answers and Congress formed a committee to investigate the unprofitabllility of the factories. They sifted through mountains of records and interviewed lines of witnesses. McKenney was on the spot and had to testify, but the committee found no corruption, just "inexplicable" losses. The factory system just failed, the committee concluded, but it needed to be studied "not only as a matter of curious history, but for the lesson it teaches to succeeding legislators."[45]

Astor, meanwhile, continued to expand and prosper. New companies entered the fur trade during the 1820s and existing ones continued to challenge Astor. The competition was keen and Astor's volume of business varied from place to place. In Green Bay, for example, he was a small trader; in Chicago he dominated fur traffic. In the newly settled Great Plains and Rocky Mountains, he often formed partnerships with existing companies. In the Michigan Territory, the Hudson's Bay Company was Astor's ever-present rival. The American Fur Company, however, remained the largest firm in the field after the factories were closed. Astor, better than any American before him, had mastered the complex accounting and organization needed to conduct a worldwide business.[46]

Astor always knew he had to please the Indians to stay on top. He rarely showed affection for them, but he respected them as suppliers and consumers. Their tastes dictated what he bought; their labor dictated what he sold. Indians were usually shrewd traders and Astor built his business assuming they would stay that way. Lewis Cass and William Clark, who spent much of their lives working among Indians, made this report to Congress:

> Contrary to the opinion generally entertained, they [the Indians] are good judges of the articles which are offered to them. The trade is not that system of fraud which many sup-

pose. The competition is generally sufficient to reduce the
profits to [a] very reasonable amount, and the Indian easily knows the value of the furs in his possession; he knows also
the quality of the goods offered to him, and experience has
taught him which are best adapted to his wants.[47]

By the late 1820s and into the 1830s, the fur trade had begun to
decline. Astor always knew the trade couldn't flourish forever—furs
were being collected faster than new animals were growing them.
More than scarce animals, changing tastes slowed down business. As
Astor noted from Paris in 1832, "they make hats of silk in place of
Beaver." The Industrial Revolution and the popularity of cheap,
mass-produced clothing also shut down markets for furs. "[M]any articles of manufacture which are now very low can be used in place of
deer skins & furs," Astor observed in 1823. "[T]hey receive of course
the preference."[48]

Just when Astor was wounded by mass production and new fashions, the U. S. government put a tourniquet around his neck. First, to
protect the budding American textile industry, Congress passed a tariff on English imports. That meant Astor had to pay more for British
woolen blankets, which were prized by the Indians. The Hudson's Bay
Company, of course, as a British company, imported the blankets
duty-free into Canada and used them in trade against Astor in the
Great Lakes area.[49]

Second, Congress shut the faucet on the flow of liquor into Indian
territory. Astor would have willingly turned the handle himself if other
traders would have agreed to leave it off. But as long as so many Indians
wanted whiskey, there would always be American and British traders
who would supply it. Astor met with George Simpson from the
Hudson's Bay Company to try to work out a mutual agreement to quit
trading liquor, but nothing binding was worked out.[50]

Third, congressmen evicted his labor supply, or at least rearranged it. In 1830, they voted to remove about 100,000 eastern Indians to the Great Plains area. Astor's major depots at Detroit and Mackinac Island lost many of their long-time suppliers and the central place of the fur trade in early Michigan history came to an end.[51]

These three interventions by government badly damaged Astor's fragile position in a competitive market. What must have especially galled him was that a key person behind two of these policies was his old rival, Thomas McKenney. Having been ousted as Superintendent of Indian Trade in 1822, McKenney resurfaced in government two years later. His old friend John C. Calhoun waited until the furor over the factories died down and then slipped McKenney into the War Department as senior clerk in the bounty land office. Then in March 1824, with Congressional approval, Calhoun created the Bureau of Indian Affairs with almost 100 employees—agents, interpreters, clerks, and copyists—and Thomas McKenney as superintendent.[52]

As head of the Bureau of Indian Affairs, McKenney continued his program to reform Indian culture. In his letters to Cherokees, Choctaws, Creeks, and others he often addressed them as "My Children." The government agent was their "Father." McKenney was their "Father in Washington," and the secretary of war was the "Great War Chief." Those who criticized the government were "bad birds." At least one Indian agent complained that these letters weakened his influence. But McKenney believed that "Indians are only children and require to be nursed, and counselled, and directed as such."[53]

McKenney's plans to nurse, counsel, and direct the Indians ran headlong into Astor's plans to employ them in the fur trade. The liquor issue was a major point of dispute. In 1824, Congress passed a law—one McKenney had long advocated—which required government Indian agents, not traders, to choose the places where the fur trade would be conducted. The idea here was that if Indian agents controlled the trading posts they could stop liquor from being traded.

McKenney defended the need to keep trade "within the eye of the officers of the Government," but Astor and his staff disagreed. How could
they trade furs in the most economical way if government dictated to
them where to trade and what not to trade? Robert Stuart, Astor's manager on Mackinac Island, called the law "truly a curiosity unless it originated in the fertile brain of Mr. McKinnie [sic]; but if so, it is perfectly reconcilable with the rest of his blundering absurdities."[54]

The Indian removal plan, which McKenney helped sponsor, was
even more damaging to Astor. McKenney argued that new land and a
fresh start free of whiskey would help the Indians assimilate into white
culture. He called the Indian removal plan "one of the kindest that has
ever been perfected." Astor and the Indians dissented; they didn't want
to be forced to change their ways of life and business. But McKenney
worked hard to help negotiate treaties that sent Cherokees, Choctaws,
and Chippewas, among others, moving westward.[55]

In 1834, three years before Michigan became a state, Astor quit the
fur business and sold the American Fur Company. The new silk hats,
the factory clothes, and the government restrictions on where he could
trade, what he could trade, and where Indians would live all told him
it was time to leave. Also, Astor was 71 years old and ready to do less
strenuous work. The same skills that made him America's largest fur
trader also made him profits in New York real estate. For many years,
he had been buying lots in northern Manhattan, developing the property, and selling it at a profit. This he continued to do. He also invested in the Park Theatre, the Mohawk and Hudson Railroad Company,
and the Astor House Hotel. By the time of his death in 1848, he had
accumulated America's largest fortune, about $10 million.[56]

The last years of McKenney's life were not so pleasant. Andrew
Jackson fired him as Superintendent of Indian Affairs and that ended
McKenney's career in government. Outside of government,
McKenney floundered and he spent much of the rest of his life trying

to get back in. He had no business skills, so he turned to writing and lecturing on American Indians. He published a three-volume *History of the Indian Tribes of North America* and his memoirs, but they sold few copies. He always had trouble managing money. His wife died; his son became a wastrel; and McKenney lived out of his suitcase, borrowing money and moving from city to city. In 1859 he died, at age 73, destitute, in a Brooklyn boarding house.[57]

Stevens T. Mason, the "Boy Governor," put the state of Michigan on the map, but his blunders in building state-funded railroads taught a new history lesson about limiting the role of government.

2

Governor Stevens T. Mason and Michigan's First Railroads

O N JULY 12, 1831, PRESIDENT ANDREW JACKSON, WHO WAS NO prankster, did something that made many people laugh, some curse, and others rub their eyes in disbelief. He appointed a teenager, Stevens T. Mason, to be secretary and acting governor of the Michigan Territory.[1]

Surely, the critics wondered, this was the worst case of political patronage ever seen. But during the next ten years the youthful Mason would often vindicate Jackson's judgment. Mason went from acting governor to elected governor. He plotted the strategy that brought Michigan into the Union; he made deals that defined Michigan's boundaries on two peninsulas; and he led the fight to save lives during Detroit's major cholera epidemics.

Unfortunately, he also launched a gigantic scheme of state-run railroads and canals that almost bankrupted the state. As a result,

Michigan voters went to the polls *en masse* to make their state a haven for free enterprise for the rest of the century.[2]

The Mason story begins in Virginia on the plantations of a great colonial dynasty. During the 1600s and 1700s, generation after generation of Masons led America from the battlefields of war to the halls of Congress. John T. Mason, the father of Stevens, hobnobbed with senators and even presidents on or near his 1,000 acre estate in Loudon County, Virginia. He graduated from William and Mary, married the daughter of Professor David Moir, and could have lived comfortably among family and friends for the rest of his life. The birth of his son Stevens T. Mason III in 1811 on the family plantation seemed to cement the Mason clan to Virginia.[3]

But John Mason had an adventurous spirit, a desire to move west and make his own success. In 1812, he packed up his family, crossed the Cumberland Gap, and traveled to Lexington, Kentucky. He had family nearby because his sister Catherine had married William T. Barry, a Kentucky congressman. The chase for riches, however, not political offices, was what drove Mason. He bought 300 acres of land and a country mansion. He practiced law, bought real estate, and joined his brother-in-law on the board of the Lexington branch of the Bank of the United States.

In this setting, young Stevens Thomson Mason—who was called Tom—grew up with slaves to pamper him and a family to teach him. What everyone quickly discovered was that Tom was a child prodigy. He absorbed knowledge like a sponge and could repeat verbatim highly detailed information months later. When his grandfather Moir, the professor, discovered that Tom could learn and recall almost anything, he decided to feed facts to Tom as quickly as he could digest them.

Tom breezed through the lesson on "A is for apple" and moved into the declension of Latin nouns. Soon he could trace Caesar's battle routes and recount the history of Virginia. By age seven, he could debate the merits of the Second Bank of the United States with guests of the Mason's. By age eight, young Tom had completed most of the entrance requirements to enter Transylvania University in Lexington. That year, 1819, General Andrew Jackson passed through Kentucky and visited the Mason family. Tom, who already knew the Battle of New Orleans intimately, astounded Jackson with his depth of knowledge. Jackson laid on the couch, toddy in hand, amazed at the lad who was talking to him. He would long remember that remarkable prodigy from the bluegrass of Kentucky.

Tom avoided the common trap of child prodigies: a haughty spirit and poor social skills. He was shy, congenial, and empathetic. He could listen as well as talk. Everyone—brothers, sisters, and slaves—seemed to like him. He spent a year at a private school and this helped him mix with others and set goals. He would be a governor some day, he was told, so he must train to be a leader of men, not just a master of facts.

When Tom was eight, his path to fame was detoured by hard times in the family. His father John invested all he had in an iron foundry near Mt. Sterling. Kentucky, he believed, would be the center of America's future industrial growth. Unfortunately, his business partners were swindlers, and John was almost bankrupted. The mansion, the land, and most of his slaves were sold. He lost his directorship on the Bank of the United States. The Masons rented Henry Clay's home in Lexington for almost three years while Clay was in Washington as secretary of state. But even this proved to be too much for the Masons to maintain. Tom, age 15, spent one year at Transylvania University, but had to come home to work in a grocery store to help make ends meet.[4]

John's brother-in-law, William T. Barry, came to the rescue. Barry led the Democratic party in Kentucky and helped Andrew Jackson carry the state and nation in the hotly contested presidential election in 1828. With Jackson in power, Barry was brought into the cabinet as postmaster general. He used his clout with Jackson to get John Mason appointed to a political post, something that paid well, something he could do without much effort. The president went down the list of patronage jobs and settled on Secretary of the Michigan Territory. Mason, of course, knew nothing about Michigan, but that was fine. He could learn from Lewis Cass, the territorial governor and a strong Jackson supporter.[5]

In 1830, the Masons moved to Michigan. Detroit, with its coarse fishermen, fur-trapping Indians, and tobacco-chewing backwoodsmen, was a far cry from a Virginia plantation or even a Kentucky iron foundry. With its 2,200 people, Detroit was the political hub of the bustling Michigan Territory.[6]

John Mason worked at the capitol, then in Detroit, and Tom, now 18, tagged along to help. John was no politician and soon grew bored with his job. Tom, however, flourished. He ran errands, greeted visitors, and copied letters. Governor Cass marveled at Tom's amazing retentive skills and efficient office work. Cass was a veteran Michigan politician and from him young Tom learned the basics of Michigan politics as quickly as he once had learned Caesar's battle tactics.[7]

After a year in Michigan, John was restless again and wanted to move to Texas, where he had inherited some land. He would ultimately live most of the rest of his life in Texas, chasing elusive dreams of fame and fortune. But he loved his family and needed his salary in Michigan to support them. In July 1831, President Jackson, whose cabinet was in disorder, came up with a stunning solution: Cass would come to Washington as secretary of war; John Mason would go to Texas and seek his fortune; and Tom Mason—age 19 years, 8 months, and 28 days—would be the new territorial secretary and acting governor! Young Tom was clearly overwhelmed but he went to Washington, where Jackson spent several days with him, doting on him, and treating him like a son. "Now Tom, write to me," urged the president. "I'll back you to the limit, boy. Assert your authority and if you get into trouble, *notify me!*" Just to make sure Michigan knew Jackson meant business, he sent Mason back with a large autographed document bearing the Great Seal of the United States that confirmed his appointment.[8]

Mason may have later wished Jackson had given him a dozen bodyguards instead. The sensational news of Jackson's decision reached Michigan before Mason returned. The *Detroit Journal* said it was "startled." "We could hardly credit the evidence of our senses," the editor said. Others wanted to take action. The largest public meeting to date in the history of Detroit assembled and the angry mob there shouted and waved their fists: Who was this teenager Mason, and why had Jackson dumped him in Michigan to play governor? Not only was this an insult, it was illegal—the quaint territorial constitution of Michigan required governors to be adults.[9]

Some prominent citizens feared a riot and only stilled the mob by promising to interview Mason and urge him to resign. Sensing the spirit of the city, the *Detroit Free Press* wrote that Mason, "*if* he lives to the month of October next, [will] be twenty years of age and no more. . . ."[10]

When Mason arrived in Detroit, he showed he was tactful as well as smart. Yes, he told the prominent citizens, as they could see he was only 19, but the president knew that, too, and had confidence that Mason could do the job. Moreover, the Constitution of the United States, which allows the president to appoint territorial officers, had precedence over any territorial constitution.[11]

Having answered the legal arguments, Mason asked for their advice and guidance. Would they help him to lead Michigan? He asked this question one on one to influential people throughout the territory. For example, he traveled on horseback to Mt. Clemens to ask Judge Christian Clemens, a key leader, for his help. Judge Clemens said, "Go

Courtesy of the State Archives of Michigan

Mason used his youth to his advantage and won over the elderly influential politicians by asking for advice and counsel.

to it, boy. Do what is right. Up here, we'll back you." And so did many others elsewhere. "Youth yields to advice," Mason wrote to the *Detroit Free Press*, "age seldom or never."[12]

The "Boy Governor," as he later came to be called, thus turned his age to his advantage. He spent many evenings during the next few years in the fashionable bar at Uncle Ben Woodworth's Steamboat

Hotel, listening—or at least pretending to listen—to Detroit's politicians. He showed that when pink-cheeked youths cry for advice, few graybearded elders—even sober—can say no.

Even when Jackson appointed a new governor, George B. Porter, young Mason remained in Detroit as a key advisor. When Porter died in office in 1834, Mason again took charge as acting governor.[13] By his wit and force of personality, Mason persuaded most territorial leaders that he had the ability to govern.

Seven generations of Masons in America had produced four major generals, three ambassadors, five U. S. Senators, three governors—and now one acting governor. But Michigan would soon learn that Mason had been studying government and the history of civilization since he was six years old. In fact, his family had contributed greatly to the debate in America about individual liberty and limited government. His great granduncle, George Mason, wrote the Virginia Declaration of Rights, which became the basis for the Bill of Rights in the U. S. Constitution. The proper sphere of government, as expressed in the U. S. Constitution, was to provide for the national defense and to promote law and order. When young Tom Mason applied these family principles to Michigan, he governed well.[14]

His first crisis was one of national defense—the Black Hawk War. The combative Black Hawk, chief of the Sauks, was a veteran of many wars with the white men. From his reservation in northern Illinois, he began to lead Indian raids on farms and villages near Chicago. When he urged Indians in Michigan to join him, Mason sprang into action. He called out the territorial militia, and 300 men volunteered and marched toward Chicago. Some were called back; others skirmished with Indians in Illinois and the western part of the Michigan Territory. During this fighting, Black Hawk was captured and the "war" quickly ended. The Boy Governor, meanwhile, won praise for decisive action in protecting state borders.[15]

Mason's second crisis was one of law and order: the cholera outbreak of 1832. As a major port, Detroit was vulnerable to epidemics. No one knew much about disease control and the open sewers flowing through the city were as dangerous as they were smelly. During 1832, a cholera plague blighted Detroit and claimed the lives of 10 percent of its residents. With death and disease everywhere, wardens rang bells and pushed carts up and down the streets each night, collecting dead bodies and dumping them in ditches dug throughout the city. The cholera was so contagious that sometimes the wardens began their journey healthy, contracted the plague along their routes, and died before they could finish filling the graves. Soon panic struck and it was every man for himself. The sick were abandoned; survivors fled to the countryside; and towns near Detroit blocked their roads to prevent any infected person from coming in.[16]

With law and order threatened, Mason took swift action. First, he offered the top floor of the capitol building as a hospital. Then he worked day and night to keep the roads to and from Detroit open so that medicine, food, and supplies could reach the ravaged city. When, for example, the town of Pontiac blocked its road to Detroit, Mason ordered the barriers removed. When Ypsilanti did the same thing, Mason went there personally on horseback, and fired the deputy sheriff when he refused to reopen the road. Mason galloped into towns throughout the territory opening roads, tending the sick, and securing medicine for Detroit. When winter came and the plague subsided, Michiganians talked long and often of the Boy Governor riding into towns and risking his life to restore order and confidence in the territory.[17]

Mason's effective use of government had won him praise from people throughout the territory. With his likeable personality, he made the transition easily from child prodigy to popular governor. He opened his mansion to visitors and socialized with citizens on the street. Tall and thin, Mason had dark brown hair, black eyebrows, and a dimple on his chin. He was a handsome figure out in public, walking erect and wearing his customary black broadcloth coat and silk hat. He seemed at ease whether he was reading Adam Smith's treatise on the wealth of nations, discussing politics at Uncle Ben Woodworth's Steamboat Hotel, or talking to children on the streets of Detroit.[18]

As a prodigy, Mason was eloquent as a speaker and writer. He commanded authority when he talked about the "petty emoluments" of his job, the "pecuniary embarrassments" of the state's budget, or the "devastations perpetrated by the enemy in violation of express stipulations" in a recent war. Other times, people would be jolted by the reality that their governor was not yet an adult. During the winters, he liked to slide down the banks of the Detroit River on a child's sled. And in 1833, his pregnant mother gave him another sister. Visitors, dignitaries, and reporters came to Detroit to meet this boy governor and find out why he was so effective. A look at the record showed that he boldly and energetically did those things that a governor in a limited government was supposed to do.[19]

Mason's daring leadership in the cholera scare helped prepare him to guide Michigan into statehood. The Northwest Ordinance of 1787 set up the rules for new states in the Northwest Territory to enter the Union. Mason followed them carefully: He ordered a population count; he directed the writing of the state constitution; and he surveyed the Michigan boundaries. Mason boldly took the initiative in promoting Michigan statehood, rather than waiting for Congress to act.[20]

The most dramatic episode in Mason's labors was the boundary dispute with Ohio. At stake was control of the city of Toledo and the mouth of the Maumee River. According to the Northwest Ordinance, state boundaries would follow a line from the southern tip of Lake Michigan eastward to Lake Erie. Such a line barely put Toledo in

Michigan. Ohio, which was settled before Michigan, found this appalling. When Ohioans prepared to enter the Union in 1803, they used creative cartography and, presto, their boundary shifted northward and Toledo was in Ohio. Later, in preparing for Michigan statehood, Mason studied the surveys, exposed Ohio's trickery, and claimed the "Toledo strip" for Michigan. Mason then appealed to the U. S. Supreme Court. And while he waited to hear from Washington, he used his powers to enforce the Northwest Ordinance. He organized the state militia, led them into Toledo, and sent local officeholders there scrambling for safety.[21]

President Jackson watched this "Toledo War" nervously. The 1836 elections were near and he wanted Ohio's 21 electoral votes for his

Courtesy of the State Archives of Michigan

Rather than wait for Congress to act, Mason took the initiative to promote statehood. Michigan's election of 1835 is rendered above.

hand-picked successor, Martin Van Buren. The Michigan Territory, with no electoral votes, had put him on the spot; he asked Mason to wait and let Congress settle the dispute. Mason, however, knew that

Ohio's maneuvering would tempt Congress to twist the law—and so he disobeyed Jackson, jeopardized his career, and insisted that the Northwest Ordinance be followed. "I owe Jackson everything," Mason said, "but even the president must execute the duly voted laws of the nation. . . . I will submit to my fate without a murmur."[22]

Jackson loved Mason as a son, so he said, but he loved Ohio's electoral votes even more. Therefore, he fired Mason. The president, according to Lewis Cass, had "tears in his eyes" when he did so. "That young hotspur governor," Jackson blurted, and he gave Toledo to Ohio and political novice John Horner to Michigan as a new territorial governor.[23]

Mason was out of office, but his courage made him more popular than ever in Michigan. He was cheered on the streets, toasted in the bars, and honored by the Detroit City Council. The same men who howled with rage when he was appointed, now praised him in print for the "able and satisfactory manner in which he had discharged his office. . . ." By contrast, the new governor, John Horner, was booed and hissed after he arrived in Michigan. What was worse, the staff in the capitol ignored him. While Horner tried to get somebody somewhere to listen to him, all of Michigan, it seemed, still called Mason "governor" and doted on his every act.[24]

The political deadlock was broken in 1835 when the Michigan Territory held its first election under its new constitution. The results were a landslide and the Boy Governor became Boy Governor again. The befuddled Horner, after a pep talk from Mason, left for Wisconsin to try his luck there as territorial governor.[25]

Once in office again, Mason had to reformulate his plans for Michigan statehood. He used his skills and the power of his office to negotiate the best deal for Michigan that he could. The sooner Michigan became a state, the sooner it could receive a share of the surplus that the federal treasury had remarkably amassed back in the

1830s. Jackson was fine as long as Ohio got Toledo. As a compromise, Mason traded Michigan's claim on the Toledo strip for the western section of the Upper Peninsula. With Mason and Jackson both peeved but pacified, Michigan entered the Union in January 1837, one state but two peninsulas.[26]

With Michigan in the U. S. at last, Governor Mason, at age 26, already had a fuller and more remarkable career than most retired politicians. On the standard government issues of defending state borders and preserving law and order, Mason was tenacious. His activism had paid off. But the issue of economic development, which was next on his agenda, was very different. Economic development involves the issues of freedom, creativity, and producing wealth. By contrast, defending borders and preserving law and order involve the mobilization of power to enforce existing rules. In one case, a creator is needed, in the other an enforcer. The earlier failure of the government-operated fur company showed Michigan what could happen when government tried to be a creator instead of an enforcer.[27]

Mason, with his encyclopedic mind, no doubt knew about the government debacle in fur and carefully considered its implications for his administration. Would Mason, as governor, stick to enforcing the laws, or would he move the government into economic development? The event that would shape Mason's thinking on this subject—and that of millions of other Americans as well—was the digging of a long ditch in western New York in the 1820s.[28]

The Erie Canal, which was a remarkable work of engineering, had an astounding impact on American thinking. Here we had a canal 364 miles long that connected the Great Lakes with the Atlantic coast—and it was funded not by entrepreneurs but by the state of New York. Suddenly New York City could trade with farms and cities throughout the midwest. Profits from tolls flowed into the state and the whole Great Lakes region was open to settlement and trade.[29]

Shortly after 1825, tens of thousands of New Yorkers and New Englanders filtered into Michigan via the Erie Canal. Mason himself used the Erie Canal eagerly when he had to go to and from Washington to see President Jackson. Almost everyone in Michigan gushed with praise for this new canal, which brought them immigrants and took their exports. The message seemed obvious: States that wanted to get ahead needed active governments to tax their citizens and build a transportation network.[30]

To compete with New York, for example, Pennsylvania spent $14.6 million on its Main Line Canal from Philadelphia to Pittsburgh. Maryland and Massachusetts joined in the rush with a variety of state-supported projects. Illinois and Indiana began elaborate canal networks in 1837, just when Michigan entered the Union. Railroads were being built, too, and some states began to lay track and buy locomotives.[31]

To Governor Mason this was all exhilarating. Maybe the traditional theory of limited government was wrong. Maybe states could be creators, at least in the area of transportation. And after all it was states, not the federal government, which were building these canals. That distinction might have satisfied Great Granduncle George Mason.[32]

Even as territorial governor, Mason urged Michigan to lay the foundation for the state to build internal improvements. When delegates met in 1835 to write the Michigan Constitution, they—with Mason's encouragement—wrote the following into law:

> Internal improvements shall be encouraged by the government of this state; and it shall be the duty of the legislature, as soon as may be, to make provisions by law for ascertaining the proper objects of improvement, in relation to [roads], Canals, and navigable waters. . . .[33]

In other words, Michigan's Constitution almost required the state to fund internal improvements.

After this constitution was adopted, Mason publicly supported an activist state government. "The spirit and enterprise which has arisen among our citizens, if fostered and encouraged by the [s]tate, cannot fail to lead to lasting prosperity," Mason said. By 1837, three weeks before Michigan entered the Union, Mason was more urgent: "The period has arrived when Michigan can no longer, without detriment to her standing and importance as a state, delay the action necessary for the development of her vast resources and wealth." He was also optimistic: "[W]e cannot fail soon to reach that high destiny which awaits us. I . . . demand immediate legislative action."[34]

Mason wanted to proceed effectively. He knew that legislative dickering could stifle meritorious state action. Therefore, he urged the legislature to create a Board of Internal Improvements to survey routes and choose locations. He believed that such a board of experts would avoid "extravagant, unprofitable, and useless expenditures."[35]

With Mason leading the cheers, the legislature met and almost unanimously passed an elaborate internal improvements bill. Democrats and Whigs alike joined in the public support for it. When the alternate strategy of private ownership came up, Mason recommended that the canals and railroads "should never be beyond at least the partial control of the state." "Extortion from the public" was what Mason called one bill to charter a private railroad. Most Michiganians seemed to agree. The *Detroit Daily Advertiser* noted that "Dewitt Clinton . . . built the [Erie] Canal with the funds of the state. What would be thought of the policy of surrendering that great work to the control of a private corporation[?]"[36]

The example of the Erie Canal had become the ace that trumped all opposing arguments. And if one state subsidy was good, two must be better, and three better yet. Michiganians were so confident that state projects would flourish that they promised to build two railroads from Lake Erie to Lake Michigan, and a couple of major canals across the state as well.[37]

Mason thought the state should spend $5 million to build these projects. Actually, the $5 million was just start-up money. As soon as the anticipated tolls started pouring in—as happened with the Erie Canal—the state could then build more. The legislature approved the $5 million that Mason suggested for the state projects. Then the legislature authorized the governor to negotiate a $5 million loan with the lender of his choice under the best terms he could get, as long as he didn't exceed an interest rate of 5 1/4 percent. The state, in this arrangement, would issue bonds for the $5 million and pay them back as tolls came in from the railroads and canals.[38]

Bad luck was the first problem to strike. The national economy went into a tailspin—the Panic of 1837—and capital was hard to borrow. Then came distractions. Mason talked with investors and studied the bond market in New York. During his discussions, he became sidetracked by Julia Phelps, the daughter of a wealthy leather merchant, Thaddeus Phelps. Mason courted and married her in 1838.[39]

Then came bad judgment. Businesses were failing because of the panic and most sound investors wanted more than 5 1/4 percent for their money. Mason finally persuaded the officers of the Morris Canal and Banking Company, a reputable firm, to buy the Michigan bonds. They promised to pay him the $5 million in regular $250,000 installments over several years. Mason gave them the bonds and went back to Michigan with their promise. The Morris Company then turned most of the bonds over to the Pennsylvania Bank of the United States, which then sent them to Europe as collateral for its own investments. Within three years, both the Morris Company and the Pennsylvania Bank went broke, which left Michigan with a $5 million debt scattered among European investors.[40]

An even greater disaster was the projects Michigan built. First was a canal that was to begin in Clinton Township near Detroit and move 216 miles west to Kalamazoo. This Clinton-Kalamazoo Canal began with high hopes and much fanfare. Governor Mason broke ground in Mt. Clemens in 1838 to celebrate the digging of the canal. Bands, parades, speeches, and a 13-gun salute commemorated the occasion. Then came reality. The Board hired different contractors for each mile of the canal and these contractors each had different ideas on how to build it.   One thing they all did wrong was to make the canal only 20 feet wide and four feet deep—too shallow for heavy freight and too narrow for easy passing.[41]

After seven years, and only 16 miles of digging, the ledger for the unfinished canal read: "Expenses $350,000, Toll Receipts $90.32." With funding scarce, the Board decided sometime around 1843 to cut its losses, abandon the canal, and focus on the two railroads. When construction on the canal stopped, some workers went unpaid and they stole materials from the three locks on the canal. Soon even the completed parts of the canal were ruined.[42]

The two railroads also had problems. The Michigan Central was to go from Detroit west through Ann Arbor, Jackson, and Kalamazoo and on to St. Joseph on Lake Michigan. Boats at St. Joseph could then take freight or passengers to and from Chicago. The route went through prosperous wheat farms and the state's larger cities, but poor construction and management of the road drained most of its profits each year.

The Central was built with strap-iron rails, which consisted of thin strips of iron strapped onto wooden rails. These rails were too fragile to carry heavy loads. Rather than switch to the more expensive and durable T-rails, the Board chose to run regular heavy shipments over the existing tracks and repair them frequently. Not only was this practice dangerous, it was more costly to the state in the long run.[43]

Robert Parks, who wrote a detailed book on Michigan's railroads, found a deplorable situation on the Central:

[O]verloaded locomotives were run at twice the recommended safe speed. Under the strain of continuous operation and jarring impact of high speed on strap-iron rails,
locomotives and cars were shaken to pieces, and the cost of
operation mounted dramatically. Rails were broken and
timbers crushed under the heavy loads bouncing over their
surface.

By 1846, the Central had been extended only to Kalamazoo. It had
technically been profitable each year, but did not earn enough to pay
for needed repairs and new rails.[44]

The second railroad, the Michigan Southern, was to parallel the
Central in the southern tier of counties from Monroe to New Buffalo.
Financially, the Southern was a stunning failure. It had the same problem as the Central with heavy loads on strap-iron rails. What's worse,
the Southern was built poorly: The roadbed was shaky and the curves
too sharp for locomotives.

Monroe, on Lake Erie, proved to be too shallow a port for heavy
freight to enter or exit. Also, the towns west of Monroe were too small
to send much traffic on the Southern. By 1846, the railroad had only
reached Hillsdale, about half way across the state. It had cost over $1.2
million to build that far and its earnings were small. The road did little
to move goods or people across the state; it drained capital that could
have been used more wisely.[45]

Michigan spent almost $4 million on the Clinton-Kalamazoo Canal,
the Michigan Central, and the Michigan Southern. The state also
spent about $70,000 surveying the Michigan Northern Railroad, from
Port Huron to Lake Michigan, before abandoning it. The state also
spent $47,000 clearing the route for a canal and turnpike near
Saginaw. Officials soon quit the project and the materials "either rot-
ted or were expropriated by local residents."[46]

Many of these problems occurred after Mason was governor, but he received most of the blame because he had touted the projects and signed the loan. In 1837, he narrowly won reelection as governor, but in 1839 his Whig critics were loud and brutal. Mason chose not to seek a third term. By that year he had begun to consider that the problems with the projects were more than just bad luck or poor management. Maybe the state should never have drifted into economic development. In Mason's final address as governor, he said,

> [T]he error, if error there is, was the emanation of that false spirit of the age, which forced states, as well as individuals, to over-action and extended projects. If Michigan has over-tasked her energies and resources, she stands not alone, but has fallen into that fatal policy, which has involved in almost unparalleled embarrassments so many of her sister states. Now, however, the period has arrived, when a corrective should be applied to the dangers which seem to surround her.[47]

A "false spirit of the age" Mason said, may have moved states into the "fatal policy" of funding state projects. Michigan had too many railroads and canals and too few people to pay for them.

But in a state-supported system this result, as Mason had begun to realize, would have been hard to avoid. The funding must come through the legislature, and the legislators naturally wanted projects in their districts. Jobs and markets were at stake. Some historians have suggested that if the Michigan Central had been the only project built, the strategy of state funding might have worked. But this was politically impossible. The legislators in the towns along the Central—Detroit, Ann Arbor, and Kalamazoo—needed votes elsewhere to have their railroads built. And the price for these votes was a commitment to build canals in Mt. Clemens and Saginaw and a railroad in Monroe and Hillsdale.[48]

Mason actually saw this problem early and tried to stop it by centralizing power in a Board of Internal Improvements. The Board's decisions, however, proved to be just as politically motivated as the legislature's. First, many legislators pressured (and possibly bribed) those on the Board. Second, some of the Board members secretly made money building the projects.[49]

The story of Levi Humphrey is a case in point. Mason appointed Humphrey, a key Democrat in the state, to the Board of Internal Improvements. When Humphrey took bids for constructing the Michigan Southern, he manipulated the results to assure that his friends in the firm of Cole and Clark won the contracts. Cole and Clark then charged three to four times the market price for supplies. When the complaints reached the legislature, Cole and Clark used some of their profits to bribe witnesses. The Whigs complained loudly, but when they won the governorship in 1839, they did not do much better. In 1840, the Board overspent its budget and covered it by falsifying its records.[50]

Much of the problem with the Board and the politicians was not just corruption. It was human nature. They did not spend state money as wisely as they would have spent their own. If Governor Mason, for example, had been a wealthy industrialist, would he have invested $5 million of his own money with bankers he hardly knew during a national depression? Would any of the legislators have done so?

The spending policies of the Board raise similar questions. In 1838, for example, the Board had a bridge built over the River Rouge. The problem was that the bridge they decided to build could not carry heavy freight. The Central, not the builders, lost almost ten thousand dollars that year hauling passengers and freight around the bridge. Since no individual owned the bridge, no one had a direct financial stake in building it well—or even protecting it. Not surprisingly, the next year an arsonist destroyed the bridge.[51]

In another example, the Board ordered iron spikes for the Michigan Southern in 1841. The contractors, however, only put one spike in every other hole along the track. They stole the rest of the spikes and, when questioned, they persuaded the Board that the unused spikes were defective. The Board did not own the spikes, or even have to ride on the rickety railroad that resulted; they simply believed the contractors and left the track partly unspiked.[52]

The Boy Governor, no longer a boy, left office in 1840 at age 28. He had served almost nine years as secretary, acting governor, or elected governor. During this time, he had focused so intently on administration that he had left office almost penniless.

He decided to leave Michigan for New York City, his wife's home, and make his fortune there in law and business. As he entered Buffalo, and made his way across the Erie Canal to New York City, he may have wondered why the experiment with an active government worked so much better in New York than in Michigan.

During the next two years, however, if Mason studied local politics, he saw New York repeat Michigan's experience. State legislators in districts outside the Erie Canal area had won eight new canal projects at a cost of $9.4 million. These new canals failed miserably and caused an economic collapse in the state, forcing eight banks to close and new taxes to be imposed.[53]

Pennsylvanians did even worse. They spent $14.6 million on a risky canal from Philadelphia to Pittsburgh. The large losses on it each year helped force the state into default on its bonds. Several other states also defaulted on their internal improvement bonds, which damaged U. S. credit abroad and made Michigan look better. How much attention Mason paid to this we don't know. The Boy Governor—who survived the wrath of Andrew Jackson, the raids of Black Hawk, and a deadly cholera epidemic—died of scarlet fever on January 5, 1843 at age 31.[54]

Mason was gone, but his "false spirit of the age" speech in 1840 had reopened the debate in Michigan on the role of the state in economic development. Right from the start, the government lost money building and operating the state's system of canals and railroads. William Woodbridge, the governor who followed Mason, first suggested selling the railroads to entrepreneurs and getting government out of the internal improvements business. At first, many resisted the privatization idea. Legislators wanted railroads in their districts at taxpayer expense; they worried that entrepreneurs would build them elsewhere.[55]

As the number of blunders on the projects began to multiply, however, more pressure came for the state to privatize. John Barry, who was elected governor after Woodbridge, echoed Mason and talked about "the spirit of the times unfortunately [becoming] the governing policy of states." Barry argued that "in extraordinary cases only . . . should a state undertake the construction of public works." He continued, "Seeing now the errors of our policy and the evils resulting from a departure from correct principle, let us with the least possible delay correct the one by a return to the other."[56]

Thomas Cooley, Michigan's most prominent lawyer in the 1800s, observed firsthand the way the state ran its railroads. He wrote about it later in a history of Michigan. "Doubts were arising in the minds of the people," Cooley wrote, "whether the State had been wise in undertaking the construction and management" of internal improvements. "These doubts soon matured into a settled conviction that the management of railroads was in its nature essentially a private business, and ought to be in the hands of individuals. By common consent it came to be considered that the State in entering upon these works had made a serious mistake."[57]

By 1846, Governor Alpheus Felch, who had followed Governor Barry, carried the day for privatization. "The business of transporting passengers and freight by railroad is clearly not within the ordinary design of state government," Felch observed. The legislature finally agreed and voted to sell the state's public works in 1846. The state took bids and sold the Central for $2 million and the Southern for $500,000. As a result, Michigan recovered 90 percent of its investment in the Central and 44 percent in the Southern. If the losses on the canals and other projects are included, the state—through this sale—recaptured about 55 percent of its total investment in internal improvements. This decision helped the state cut its bureaucracy and also avoid bankruptcy. As Governor Felch had noted, "A sale of these works would have the effect to simplify the operations of the state, to reduce the number of officers and servants in its employ, and to render less complicated the whole machinery of government."[58]

As a condition of the sale, the new railroad owners had to agree to rebuild both lines with quality rails and extend them to Lake Michigan within three years. It had taken the state nine years to move the lines not much more than half way across the state; the new entrepreneurs had to rebuild that part and complete the rest in just three years. When they did so, and kept rates competitive, too, Michiganians knew they had learned something. They moved quickly to write this discovery into law.[59]

The next year, 1850, Michigan held a state constitutional convention. The proper role of government in society was one of the issues. The 1835 constitution, which mandated government support for internal improvements, was changed. In its place was the following: "The [s]tate shall not subscribe to or be interested in the stock of any company, association, or corporation." Further, "the [s]tate shall not be a party to or interested in any work of internal improvement, nor engaged in carrying on any such work" except for the donation of land.[60]

The public debate that followed showed much support for the new constitution. "Looking at it as a whole," said the *Grand Rapids Enquirer,* "we honestly believe that if it had been adopted at the organization of our [s]tate [g]overnment, our [s]tate would now be out of debt, prosperous, and flourishing." In November 1850, the voters of Michigan overwhelmingly accepted the new constitution. Michigan had learned from its history. The building of railroads and the development of resources—lumber, copper, and chemicals—would all be done by private enterprise.[61]

Henry Crapo came to Michigan late in life to carve out a remarkable career in the lumber business. Later, as governor, he was at the center of a political storm as an opponent of railroad subsidies.

William Durant, the grandson of Henry Crapo, thrived in the carriage business before building his first Buick. After reaching the pinnacle as president of General Motors, he lost his fortune in the stock market.

3

Henry Crapo and William Durant:
From Lumber to Carriages to Cars

"TIM-BERRR!" WAS THE SOUND THAT SIGNALLED MICHIGAN'S rise as a major industrial state. The millions of pine trees that blanketed the state were transformed by lumbermen into houses, chairs, carriages, and railroad ties. In the process, jobs and capital came to Michigan and new cities like Flint, Grand Rapids, Saginaw, and Muskegon sprouted and flourished.

From after the Civil War until almost 1900, Michigan was the nation's leading producer of wood. Aggressive lumbermen there felled enough trees in the late 1800s to floor the entire state of Michigan with one-inch boards and have enough left over to plank a road 60-feet wide from Detroit to San Francisco.[1]

The success of Michigan's lumber industry was uncertain when Michigan entered the union in 1837. Many people viewed land there as a poor investment. For most of the early 1800s, Michigan had suffered from bad press. Not only was Michigan regarded as cold and remote, the experts declared it swampy and almost uninhabitable. James Monroe wrote to Thomas Jefferson that Michigan "will never contain a sufficient number of inhabitants to entitle them to membership in the confederacy."

Edward Tiffin, the surveyor-general of the United States, did a survey of Michigan after the War of 1812 and concluded that only about one acre in a hundred could be farmed. Finally, in 1822 the War Department built a fort among the vast forests of pine at Saginaw. The troops, however, contracted malaria and the post was soon abandoned. The commanding officer announced that "Indians, muskrats and bullfrogs" were all that would ever live along the Saginaw River.[2]

The presence of millions of acres of pine trees in Michigan offered the state the chance to change its image and give settlers a reason to make a right turn north when they traveled the western route through Ohio, Indiana, and Illinois. Here is an important point, however. Just because Michigan had an abundance of timber did not mean the state would prosper from it. In Maine, the trees were cut and the lumbermen and their capital promptly departed. Extractive industries are often like that. Nevada, for example, had abundant silver, but it was often used to build empires in San Francisco. In Pennsylvania, the towns of Carbondale, Pittston, and Jermyn had abundant resources of anthracite coal, but outsiders—usually in New York—mined it and spent the profits outside the coal fields.[3] In Michigan, the story would be different.

As late as 1850, few people in Michigan knew anything about harvesting timber. The white pine, which Michigan had in abundance, was an ideal wood to build with. It was soft, compact, and straight-grained, which made it easy to convert into boards. The technology for chopping down trees was primitive, consisting mainly of axes, crosscut saws, and elbow grease. Labor was scarce, and therefore had to be paid a good wage. Investment capital was hard to find and often had to come from outside the state.

The lumber industry was fraught with risks. First, it was not easy to find land that largely consisted of mature pines. Hemlocks, elms, and spruces grew along with the pines and investors had to hire timber cruisers to find the better tracts of pineland. Even if the timber cruiser did his job well, the second problem was that land surveys were sometimes unreliable and boundaries unclear. Legal squabbles could drain an investor's time as well as his cash. Third, even if he secured full title to high quality forestland, an unpredictable fire could send his investment up in smoke. Fourth, prices for logs fluctuated wildly during the early years of the lumber industry. The costs of land and labor were fairly steady, but market prices were volatile. Fifth, harvesting timber was dependent on the weather. Logs were cut in winter, skidded on ice to a nearby river, and sent down the river in the spring. Even if the choppers, sawyers, and teamsters did their jobs well, a warm winter would produce no ice to slide the logs to the river and a flash flood in the spring could disrupt the flow of logs to the port.[4]

The question, then, is this: "Why should an entrepreneur in the mid-1800s come to cold and isolated Michigan and take risks cutting and selling logs when he could invest in coal in Pittsburgh, textile mills in Boston, or iron foundries in Scranton?" Without an appealing entrepreneurial climate, he would not. The state of Michigan had to do what it could to make itself attractive to entrepreneurs and hope that some of them would come and stay. For Michigan to prosper from its pine forests four things had to happen.

First, the timberland had to be sold cheaply. With so many risks already inherent in the lumber business, entrepreneurs needed the bait of inexpensive land if they were to grab the opportunities in Michigan. During the 1850s, the federal government made available over ten million acres of land in Michigan—much of it with timber—for a reasonable $1.25 an acre. Prices rose somewhat in the 1860s and 1870s, but buyers were still able to get competitive prices for high quality pineland.[5]

This scene above is from the lumber industry. In all stages of operation, lumbering required huge amounts of capital.

Second, Michigan had to create a favorable climate for entrepreneurs. This meant low taxes, few regulations, and no special subsidies for some at the expense of others. The new state Constitution of 1850 was an excellent step in telling future entrepreneurs they would not have the government competing against them. The state promised "not [to] subscribe to or be interested in the stock of any company, association, or corporation" or to invest "in any work of internal improvement."

The tone and direction of that document made it clear that Michigan was staking its future on the abilities of entrepreneurs, not the central planning of politicians.[6]

Of course, most if not all states in the late 1800s and early 1900s tended to support limited government. But Michigan did so more than its neighbors. North Dakota, for example, supported a large state-run bank and state-operated grain elevators. Minnesota, through federal subsidies, gave large land grants to the Northern Pacific Railroad, which went bankrupt under bad management. Wisconsin challenged its entrepreneurs by adopting a statewide progressive income tax. Nebraska gave subsidies to sugar beet growers.[7] Michigan's early disaster with state-subsidized railroads made it skeptical of political solutions to economic problems, as explained in Chapter 2.

Third, Michigan needed entrepreneurs with capital to come and stay. The lumber industry was a sponge for capital at all stages of operation. Before any money came in, lumbermen needed lots of cash on hand just to feed and pay a crew to chop trees down, cut them into logs, and move them to the river. Boom companies, which sorted the logs downstream and sent them to the sawmills, also needed funding. Finally, cash was needed for operating the sawmills that took the logs, made them into boards, and sent them to market. Entrepreneurs had to fill these gaps, and it would do Michigan little good if they cut the trees down, took their profits, and moved elsewhere to invest.[8]

Fourth, Michigan had to diversify beyond using lumber for fence posts, rail ties, and new houses. As Michigan's forests disappeared, new timberland opened in areas from Wisconsin to Washington. Michigan would need to use its native lumber not always for boards, but for skilled craft products from furniture to carriages. These businesses would be more permanent and were essential to serious economic growth. In part, this meant Michigan would have to be creative and inventive: New machines would be needed to thrust deeply into the forests and shape the wood into fine products.[9]

The story of Henry H. Crapo helps show how Michigan won the fierce battle for entrepreneurs and capital during its lumber era. Crapo was a remarkable and versatile entrepreneur, but he started life in 1804 as the son of a struggling farmer in Dartmouth, Massachusetts. After his father died, he moved to New Bedford, a whaling port, and hustled real estate and sold merchandise on commission. He also became a sales agent for a plant nursery and a gauger, someone who checked local scales for accuracy. From there, he became a secretary of a large insurance company; he was also elected town clerk and tax collector, which gave him access to the richest capitalists in the area.[10]

Crapo was diligent, versatile, and ambitious. With his contacts and his skill he searched for larger investments, ones that more cautious souls might be overlooking. A land speculator from Michigan came to New Bedford and tantalized him with a 12,000-acre stand of pine near Flint for $150,000. Crapo had the land surveyed and convinced himself that he could market the lumber, sell the land for farms, and make a handsome profit. His reputation was so strong in New Bedford that he easily persuaded two wealthy townsmen to put up the capital and join him as co-investors in Michigan lumber.[11]

Crapo hoped to sit back in his New Bedford office and reap large profits each year from his timber harvest. Soon he realized he needed to be in Michigan frequently. The trees on his land were not as plentiful as he had originally thought; also the nearby Flint River had several dangerous rapids that did not easily float logs to market. What was worse, the prices for wood dropped quickly soon after he had launched his lumber career.[12]

At age 51, Crapo began to doubt the wisdom of his western investment. Now that it was done, however, he was determined to learn the lumber business and make a success of it in Michigan. "[I]f it be a mistake there is only one way ever to retrieve it," he wrote, "and that is by making the best of what remains." That meant moving to Flint to protect his investment and that of his wealthy partners who trusted him. "Unless all my powers of body and mind and all my time are devoted to my business here [in Flint]," he wrote his son, "I must inevitably lose what little I may have acquired during many years of care and anxiety and some little toil."[13]

Expanding the business, Crapo concluded, was the best way to salvage it. He built two sawmills in Flint to process his lumber and that of others. "Money is very scarce here," he wrote, "and I am in great want of every dollar I can raise." He buttonholed his partners, his family, and his friends in New Bedford for cash. "I shall be obliged to draw upon you tomorrow for funds for future expenses, as we cleaned out everything in the shape of money last night." Looking around, Crapo noticed that others in Michigan were also seeking cash in New England. "The west has entirely drained the east of money," he wrote at one point.[14]

After winning help from his somewhat anxious friends in New Bedford, Crapo pursued a two-fold strategy. First, harvest the best product at the lowest price possible. Second, try to reach markets all around the country with his lumber. To do this meant strict attention to detail. From 4:00 a.m. to 7:00 p.m., Crapo would be absorbed in the details of logging, sawing, and searching for buyers from Chicago to Albany to New Bedford. "I shall for the future," he said, "superintend personally everything in relation to the hiring of the men, the running of the mills, the manufacture of the lumber, etc. These things cannot be submitted to hired help—foremen though they be—without great loss; for men cannot be found who will for mere wages do that which an employer's interest requires."[15]

For almost six years, Crapo verged on bankruptcy. He had many competitors and prices sometimes fluctuated wildly. "The buyers of

Henry Crapo personally superintended the details of his sawmill operations.

lumber here are all sharks," he insisted. "[T]hey intend to buy of the poor manufacturer at their own prices, and sell to the dealer at . . . higher rates." Laborers also worried Crapo. "They are continually clamoring for more wages," he complained, "and the more I raise on their wages the less they do." Many lumbermen delayed paying their workers, or paid them in credit at a company store. Crapo found that when he paid his wages promptly and in cash he attracted better and more loyal workers.[16]

Crapo's hard work paid off. His lumber developed a strong reputation for quality throughout Michigan. "Mine is in fact the best lot of seasoned lumber . . . ," Crapo wrote, "that can be found anywhere in this region, and all the lumber buyers on this side of the peninsula know it." He won the business of scores of farmers and townsfolk in the Flint area and he delighted when they came to town and passed up the cheaper lumber of his competitors and came straight to his mills.[17]

Crapo's lumber was so popular locally that he had to find a way to ship it cheaper and quicker to outside markets. The existing rivers and plank roads were too slow and had too small a reach. He needed railroads, especially one that would tie Flint to outside markets. Crapo looked south toward Detroit, and began raising capital to build a line to the town of Holly, which already had a link to Detroit. "[E]verybody in Michigan expects that I am going to build . . .," Crapo wrote in 1863, "because I pay as I go along, and have succeeded in my business beyond expectation." Nothing less than $250,000 was needed to build the line and Crapo again looked eastward for help. He pitched the scheme to investors in New Bedford and Boston and, with his family's help, secured almost all the money needed from those two cities. Crapo became the president of the railroad; and when it later merged with the Flint and Pere Marquette Railroad, Crapo headed that, too.[18]

Years of hard work and attention to detail had begun to pay off for Crapo. He was poised for growth when salt factories, using local brine, began to form in the Saginaw Valley. As Michigan became the leading salt producer in the Union, Crapo flourished by sending his high quality wood to Saginaw for use in building homes and salt factories.

His reputation for quality had spread throughout eastern Michigan; he expanded his business in Flint and opened a large lumberyard in Detroit. Even the humble Crapo admitted in 1865 that his business was "immense" and that "everything in regard to it looks flattering at the present time." Three years later he wrote that "there is probably no man making lumber in this state any cheaper . . . than I am."[19]

Crapo's remarkable career in Michigan made him an ideal candidate for political office. The Republicans nominated him for mayor of Flint in 1860, and he won election easily. Two years later, the voters in

Logs going to market down the river.

the Flint area sent Crapo, their most prominent citizen, to the state senate. His strong integrity, his belief in limited government, and his business success brought him fame throughout the state. In 1864, Crapo was elected governor of Michigan, and two years later he was reelected to a second term.[20]

As governor, Crapo fought to make Michigan a haven for entrepreneurs. Low taxes and a small state government, he argued, along with vigorous promotion of Michigan as a good place to invest would help bring the right kinds of immigrants to Michigan. Others disagreed. The idea of using tax money to subsidize railroads did not die in the 1840s; it reappeared in the 1860s and Crapo had a fight on his hands. The Constitution of 1850 banned railroad subsidies by the state, but what about towns? Many cities and towns in Michigan wanted to lure private railroads through local subsidies. In Crapo's second term, the legislature passed laws that would let cities tax their people, bring in a railroad, and use it to spur economic growth.[21]

Crapo dissented and vetoed all such bills. Local governments, he argued, could not finance or subsidize any railroad because they were creatures of the state and therefore subject to the Constitution of 1850. He further argued that local aid to railroads would make taxes plentiful and entrepreneurs scarce. Had Michigan not learned from its own history the dangers of railroad subsidies? "If it be so unwise a thing on the part of the [s]tate at large," Crapo argued, "thus to engage in, or aid uncertain enterprises . . ., it must be vastly more unwise and perilous, for the feebler townships and cities, thus to . . . expose to serious hazards, their more limited credits." He concluded that local subsidies to railroads would "repel capital . . . and deter the flow of immigration. These results naturally follow in any [s]tate or community overburdened by taxation."[22]

Crapo found himself at the center of a political storm. Criticism rained upon him from town leaders and railroad investors throughout the state. From there, the turbulence split the Republican party and washed out Crapo's political career. "The railroad men outside and in the [l]egislature," Crapo observed, "have done everything that could be done to coerce members, and to manufacture public opinion against my views." To a large extent they succeeded.[23]

The next governor repudiated Crapo's stand, and legislators rushed to let their towns give subsidies to railroads. In 1871, however, the state supreme court sided with Crapo. Local aid to railroads, the judges declared, violated the Constitution of 1850—and with this verdict the issue died. Meanwhile, Crapo's health was broken. The stresses of business and politics made him chronically ill during his last years and he died in 1869, at age 65.[24]

How odd that a New Englander, one who came to Michigan late

in life, one who made his fortune in lumber and who was content with that, should be the sparkplug in defense of the Michigan Constitution. What Crapo had discovered from his own life, however, was that entrepreneurs were made, not born. Low taxes and access to credit Crapo had to have or he would never have built his lumber empire. Tax subsidies to railroads, Crapo argued, could wreck Michigan's future by chasing away entrepreneurs and cautious New England bankers. "[W]hen the exhilaration of profuse expenditures shall be succeeded by the grinding exactions of the tax-gatherer, . . ." Crapo wrote in his veto message, "I shall then, if surviving, have the melancholy satisfaction of knowing that I have endeavored . . . to avert these calamities from my fellow citizens and to maintain the rights of property. . . ."[25]

The death of Henry Crapo raised the interesting question of what his children would do with their father's business. Crapo had ten children; many of them—including his only son William—prefered to live in New Bedford. William was a talented businessman and had long helped his father tap into New England capital markets. The Henry Crapo estate was worth nearly one million dollars: Would this capital stay in Flint in lumber and railroads, would it return to New England, or would it flow toward attractive investments elsewhere?[26]

Crapo had thought of this crucial issue and had argued to his son that Michigan—whether the whole family moved there or not—was the best place to invest even with the risk that the Constitution of 1850 might be violated. As early as 1858, Henry told William, "New England, or perhaps I should say some of its older cities—New Bedford for instance—may at the present time very justly be likened to an infirm old man, who during a life of toil has enriched himself and is now under the decrepitude of old age, sitting quietly—almost helplessly— down with his pockets and coffers full of gold. Michigan, or 'the West,' may be as justly compared to a young, robust man, . . . with a physical organization perfectly developed. . . ." Before his death, Crapo asked his son to run the lumber business from New Bedford, build the estate for the rest of the family, and help Michigan, that "young robust" state, develop its resources.[27]

Like a dutiful son, William Crapo kept the family fortune in Michigan. He visited Flint regularly each year and his two brothers-in-law, Humphrey H. H. C. Smith and Harlan P. Christy, managed the lumber company in his absence. Other family members moved to Flint, too, where the Crapo name opened the doors to investment opportunities. William, meanwhile, also served as congressman

Courtesy of the GMI Alumni Historical Collection

A photo of Henry Crapo's family. When grown, Crapo's ten children— including his only son, William—preferred to live in New Bedford, Connecticut, raising the question of whether the million-dollar estate would remain in Michigan.

Courtesy of GMI Alumni Historical Collection

Rebecca Durant, daughter of Henry Crapo and mother of William Durant.

from the New Bedford area, which gave Michigan more political clout in Congress.[28]

What Henry Crapo could never have known, or even guessed, was that one of his grandsons, a child called "Willie," would one day be the catalyst to spearhead Michigan's crucial diversification of its lumber resources. "No living man," Crapo once reflected, "is, I am sensible, aware of the rapidity with which our pine forests in Northern Michigan . . . are disappearing." Grandson Willie was, and when he reached manhood he did something about it.[29]

As a teenager William Durant was popular in high school. He was a good socializer and a smart student. Nevertheless, he quit high school in his fourth year to learn about business.

The story of Willie begins with the daughters of Henry Crapo. When Crapo was scouring New England, searching for capital, he met several men whose attention turned from his bankbook to his daughters. One of these men was William Clark Durant, member of an old New England family, clerk at the Webster National Bank in Boston, and a land agent there for Henry Crapo. Durant courted and married Crapo's daughter Rebecca in 1855.[30]

At first, the match seemed an excellent one. William and Rebecca had two children, Rosa and Willie. Durant did errands for his father-in-law and helped sell stock in his Flint and Holly Railroad to Boston investors.

Crapo seems to have liked Durant, and urged "you and Becky" to visit Flint when possible. Crapo took a special liking to their son, William Crapo Durant, or "Willie." In one letter to "Master Willie," Crapo said that he "wants to have a visit from [Willie] very very much. Grand Pa knows that 'Willie' is a very fine boy, and he is very proud of him. . . ." In another letter, "Grand Pa," now governor of Michigan, asked four-year-old "Willie [to] be Grand Pa's Private Secretary. . . ."[31]

Grand Pa's affection for Willie was soon matched by his concern for his son-in-law. Durant quit his job at the bank, became a stockbroker, and began risking large sums in stocks. "[M]y advice to him," Crapo said, "was to go back into the Bank . . . and be careful about . . . the troubled and uncertain seas of stock speculation." Durant rejected this advice, went broke in the stock market, and began drinking heavily. When he came to Flint, looking for a job, Crapo tried to help him but couldn't. Durant, Crapo wrote, "has not mind enough to know what to do, and has apparently given himself up to intoxicating drinks. He can't get by a saloon or a drinking hole, no matter how low, without a 'tip'." Before a week was out, Crapo noted, "every business man in Flint knew that he was a tippler. . . ." What was worse, Durant was "so intoxicated here as to have a regular drunken jab with Rebecca at the table before us all. . . ."[32]

Governor Crapo prepared for the worst. He changed his will to ensure that Rebecca had control of her share of the inheritance. Even so, Crapo was always concerned with Willie: How would he get by?

Courtesy of the GMI Alumni Historical Collection

William Durant in his early twenties, about the time he took his first memorable carriage ride that launched him into the carriage business.

What kind of work would he do? "The habits of the boy," Crapo said, "are to be formed, both by parental training and parental example, in order to give him proper notions of business. . . ." When Willie was seven, "Grand Pa" died; his parents divorced soon afterward. Willie's father drifted from place to place and disappeared from his family's life completely. In 1872, at age ten, Willie moved to Flint with his mother to live with his prominent relatives there.[33]

Growing up in Flint, Willie had no father to imitate, but he did have uncles who were lumbermen and bankers. Willie was popular in school, a good socializer, and a smart student. He left high school in his fourth year, however, to learn about business. He worked briefly for Crapo Lumber Company, and then sold patent medicine and fire insurance. Here he found his gift as a salesman. Friends later said he could sell sand to the Arabs and then sell them sieves to sift it.

George T. Warren, a local cigarmaker, hired Willie experimentally to go on the road and sell cigars. In two days, Willie astonished Mr. Warren by selling 22,000 cigars. The experiment was over: Three other salesmen were fired and Willie was on salary for $100 a month. "Grand Pa" would have been proud.[34]

The destiny of William Durant, however, would not be in cigars or even lumber, but in carriages. It all started by accident. In 1886, young Durant, age 24, hitched a ride to the local waterworks from his friend John Alger. Durant had never ridden in a cart like Alger's before— small and durable, two four-feet wheels, two seats wide, and very smooth on bumps and turns even when the horse trotted briskly. The cart was light and graceful with a slatted footboard and a sturdy iron bar to grip for support. When the ride ended, Durant checked out the new cart. The seat was mounted to flexible springs in a way that cushioned the shock and cut the vibrations. The excited Durant, ever the salesman, envisioned himself selling these smooth-riding carts at low prices to middle-class men and women all over the nation.[35]

Quickly Durant asked Alger where he got the cart and how much it cost. The answers led him by train the next day 75 miles away to Coldwater, Michigan, and the factory of the owners of this new cart, William Schmedlin and Thomas O'Brien. After some haggling, Durant bought the company from them, patents and all, for $1,500. That was great, except that Durant had no ready cash and was $3,500 in debt from having married and bought a home the year before. He had to raise $1,500 in five days or the deal was off.[36]

Less than one day after signing papers in Coldwater, Durant was back home, standing on Saginaw Street, wondering where he would get $2,000, $1,500 for the business and $500 to bring it all to Flint. From the intersection at Saginaw and Kearsley Streets, he could see the Genesee County Savings Bank, founded and run by his Uncle James Willson, and the First National Bank of Flint, recently headed by his Uncle Ferris Hyatt. These were obvious possibilities, or he could just

Courtesy of the GMI Alumni Historical Collection

William Durant's "Blue Ribbon Vehicles."

ask Uncle William Crapo in New Bedford. The son of William Clark Durant had a problem with these family options. "If I make a failure of this venture," he thought, "I will never hear the last of it." He would need his family for capital if his business grew big enough, but right now he had to show them he was more like "Grand Pa" than "Pa."[37]

"Billy," as his friends now called him, strolled haltingly into the Citizens Bank of Flint, "not as pretentious as the others," he thought, "but sound as a rock." After a talk with President Richard Whaley, the persuasive Durant, with his customary soft voice, friendly smile, and thorough confidence, walked out with a $2,000 loan for 90 days. [38]

Courtesy of the GMI Alumni Historical Collection

William Durant and J. Dallas Dort bought up buildings throughout Flint to store their supplies and build their vehicles. Pictured here is the Durant-Dort Carriage Building.

Next, Durant needed a partner, someone to run the new business while he rounded up customers. Young J. Dallas Dort, the manager of a local hardware store, rushed to join his friend Durant in the new Flint

Snapshots taken at the Durant-Dort Carriage Company.

Road Cart Company. Dort, who bought a half interest for $1,000, would supervise the making of carts; Durant would be on the road selling them.[39]

From his first day in business, Durant looked for ways to market his cart beyond Flint, or even Michigan. When his supplies arrived from Coldwater, he took one of the two finished carts and entered it in the Tri-State Fair in Madison, Wisconsin. "I did not have to do much talking," Durant said modestly. The smooth-riding cart had strong appeal and when the competition was over it had won the blue ribbon. With this award in hand, Durant traveled to Milwaukee and Chicago and lined up jobbers to sell the carts in those cities. He had only one finished cart back in Flint, but he returned home with orders for over 600 vehicles. Furthermore, with charm and finesse, Durant managed to work out the contracts so that he would be paid quickly for carts delivered—his company was too short of cash to have much lag between sale and payment.[40]

When Durant arrived home, it's hard to know who was more surprised at his accomplishments, J. Dallas Dort, his astonished partner, or William A. Paterson, the local carriage maker, who was asked by Durant if he could make 600 carts right away. Paterson was accustomed to making only two carriages a day; Durant's massive business allowed him to to expand his factory. Even 600 carts were too few for the visionary Durant. In their contract, Paterson agreed to supply 3,200 carts for Durant in one year at $12 per cart. Durant, in turn, went from town to town hiring salesmen and selling the carts for $22. In the midst of success, Paterson, the wily veteran, double-crossed the Flint Road Cart Company. He discovered who some of Durant's buyers were and began marketing his own road cart, remarkably similar to Durant's, for only $15.[41]

Durant, however, hardly flinched from this setback: He and Dort began making as well as selling what they called their "Blue Ribbon" road carts. They bought up buildings throughout Flint to store their supplies and build their vehicles. Durant knew he could go from city to city and outsell Paterson if only Dort could supervise the business on the homefront. They were so successful that soon they diversified into carriages and farm vehicles. Their experience with Paterson taught them to make their own parts and build their own carriages. Capital from Durant's Crapo relatives and other Flint friends began to pour in and give him a base for expanding.[42]

"We started out as assemblers with no advantage over our competitors," Durant remarked. "We paid about the same prices for everything we purchased. We realized that we were making no progress and would

Courtesy of GMI Alumni Historical Collection

Pictured above are officials of the Durant-Dort Carriage Company in Flint, some of whom later became automotive pioneers. Front row (from left) are W.C. Durant, A.B.C. Hardy, W.C. Orrell, and Fred A. Aldrich. Back row (from left) are: James A. Slocum, Charles D. Wesson, and Charles Webster. In the center is J. Dallas Dort.

not unless and until we manufactured practically every important part that we used." Vertical integration is the term economists use for this method of controlling production from raw materials to distribution. And Durant used vertical integration to cut costs and keep his company supplied with axles, wheels, varnish, and lumber. He built factories in and around Flint to make these crucial ingredients in assembling carriages. He even experimented with making some parts for carriages on an assembly line.[43]

During the 1890s, the Flint Road Cart Company changed its name to Durant-Dort and began exporting carriages all over the United States, and in Canada and Australia as well. They even started a profitable mail-order business to sell their vehicles. Durant, always the imaginative marketer, discovered that Easterners preferred their carriages to be painted black, but that Midwesterners liked more variety in color, including pinstripes. Fred Aldrich, the secretary of Durant-Dort, observed, "Mr. Durant's vision, forecast and organizing ability and Mr. Dort's productive talents kept steadily onward and upward. . . ." By 1901, Durant and his friends had transformed $2,000 in start-up capital into a $2 million a year business. Durant-Dort had become the largest carriage producer in the nation, and probably the world. In 1906, their biggest year, they employed 1,000 workers, who made about 480 vehicles each day. [44]

Durant's meteoric rise in the carriage industry occurred at the same time that Michigan's timber resources were rapidly dwindling. His success inspired others to shift from lumber to carriages, and in the 1890s Michigan had about 125 carriage companies servicing the nation. Flint took the name "Vehicle City" and Michigan became a center for expertise and talent in carriage-making. Capital and talent shifted smoothly from Crapo Lumber into Durant-Dort. For example, Durant started the Victoria Vehicle Company in 1894 to make a new line of carriages. He bought the large factory space for the company from his Uncle James Willson, who founded the Genesee County Savings Bank and used it to help finance Durant. Durant in turn hired Willson's son George to manage the Victoria Company and make it profitable.[45]

As Durant-Dort grew in size, it needed help not just from the Crapos, but from the whole city of Flint. Durant's work force, for example, was loyal and able, and he did what he could to keep them that way.

Unionism touched the railroaders and cigarmakers in Flint, but not Durant. He tried to make his plant workers feel that they were part of a large family. Work hours were from 7:30 a.m. to 5:30 p.m. Monday through Saturday, and he gave them an hour and a quarter for lunch. He and his management team gave bonuses for merit, parties on holidays, and gifts at employee weddings. He even bought tickets to local baseball games for all his staff several times a year.[46]

Durant, many thought, could sell his carriages to the blind and his farm vehicles by mail order to urban illiterates. Often, however, what he was selling was simply himself and his ability to create a new product. In the 1890s, for example, Durant started a company in Flint to make bicycles. Many Flint citizens bought stock in the company simply because Durant was heading it. The bicycle craze of the 1890s, however, fizzled and Durant's company ended up losing money. When that happened, he took his profits from Durant-Dort and covered the losses of his friends, who had trusted him enough to invest their money in his bicycle venture.[47]

Durant would need help from all his family and friends when he spearheaded the transition in America from carriages to cars. During the 1890s, several mechanics had tinkered with steam, electric, and gas-powered vehicles. None had made a competitive product, however, and most carriage-makers saw no threat to their industry. Durant didn't either for awhile, but in 1904, a group of investors in Flint urged

Courtesy of the GMI Alumni Historical Collection
William Durant in 1908, which was the year he started General Motors.

him to take over production of the Buick, a local car with small sales
and large debts.[48]

At first, Durant hesitated: Cars were smelly, noisy, and dangerous.
He had even refused to let his daughter ride in one. But cars also might
be the vehicle of the future. He tested a Buick on the streets of Flint
and over the potholes of the countryside. He liked the way it ran and
he liked the challenge of building an industry from scratch. Durant
would take over the Buick if his family and friends would supply him

with capital and expertise. Immediately funds poured in from Flint's banks, especially the Crapo family's Genesee County Savings Bank. Uncle William Crapo in New Bedford joined the family fun and bought stock. Other Flint investors, including lumbermen and wagon-makers, also anted up. Durant-Dort supplied factory space, auto parts, and their sales and distribution network. Durant soon had a company capitalized at $500,000 and was in business.[49]

Courtesy of the State Archives of Michigan

The Chevrolet assembly line.

With the money and organization in place, Durant the salesman sprang into action. In 1904, he repeated his success with the road carts 18 years earlier. He entered the Buick in a New York auto show—and came home with orders for 1,108 cars, not bad considering that only 37 Buicks had ever been made. Walter Chrysler, who began his long career in carmaking with Buick, spoke for many when he said of Durant, "I cannot hope to find words to express the charm of the man.

. . . He could coax a bird right down out of a tree, I think." Durant settled for coaxing outside experts, such as New Yorker Charles Mott, into
his Flint organization to make first-rate axles. Durant also made use of
local talent, such as Arthur Mason, his plant superintendent. Mason
built for Buick an engine twice as powerful (4,000 r.p.m.) as any on the
market, and Durant made that fact a key advertising point. By 1908,
after four years in the car business, Durant had brought Buick from
near bankruptcy to being the best-selling car in America. His company
was worth $3.5 million and had the largest auto factory in the world.
The carriage king had been transformed into an auto genius.[50]

Durant and his main rival, Henry Ford, were both prescient: They
envisioned mass appeal for the car. Ford, however, thought his company should be built around one standard car, his low-priced, no frills
Model T. Durant, from his years in the carriage business, knew that in
the long run if he were to prevail as the auto leader he needed many
different types of vehicles to cater to different incomes and tastes. He
therefore scoured the country with the idea of having Buick merge
with other companies that could carve out a niche in the auto market. He bought Cadillac, for example, for its luxury cars, which
appealed to those who could afford something more expensive than
his Buicks. In 1908, Durant founded General Motors, a consolidation
of 13 car companies and 10 parts-and-accessories manufacturers,
with a capitalization of $60 million.[51]

The twentieth century has shown that Durant's vision of different
types of cars for different customers was the best way to build the
largest car company in America. His problem came when he tried to
stitch together the right automakers into his General Motors fabric.
His Buicks and Cadillacs sold steadily and profitably; most others did
not. "They say I shouldn't have bought Cartercar," Durant said later.
"Well, how was anyone to know that Cartercar wasn't going to be the
thing? It had the friction drive and no other car had it. . . . And then

there's Elmore, with its two-cycle engine. That's the kind they were using on motorboats. . . . I was for getting every kind of thing in sight, playing safe all along the line." By 1911, General Motors was losing too much money. In that year, a group of Boston stockholders ousted Durant from leadership at General Motors and ran the company cautiously—making tens of thousands of Buicks and Cadillacs and putting the Cartercars and Elmores in museums of antiquity.[52]

Durant was resilient, however. "We're going to need a car," he told his family and friends in Flint; with their capital and expertise, he started making the Chevrolet, a new economy car that quickly captured a large share of the market. Durant then cleverly traded much of his Chevrolet stock for General Motors stock, and soon held a controlling interest in both companies. In 1916, he triumphantly returned to General Motors for a final five-year term as chief executive officer.[53]

During his second presidency, Durant bought the Fisher Body Company and Frigidaire to add to his Chevrolets, Oldsmobiles, Cadillacs, and Buicks. People like Charles Kettering, who invented the self-starter, and Alfred Sloan, a brilliant organizer, joined the General Motors team—which employed almost 100,000 workers by 1920. Like Walter Chrysler, Sloan thought Durant was a genius, often guided by "some intuitive flash of brilliance" which was "at times . . . astoundingly correct."[54]

Flint, meanwhile, became the fastest growing city in the United States. It soared from 13,000 in 1900 to 91,000 in 1920. A reporter from Detroit was astounded at the building and bustle of entrepreneurship parading throughout Flint. "Whence has Durant this ability to use his boyhood village as a commercial center for the country?" he asked. "[O]ne must himself walk over the literal miles of factories in process of construction before one begins to grasp the immensity of the manufacturing undertaking that has made Flint, next to Detroit, the automobile center of the world." Durant revelled in Flint's prominence, and did what he could to bring more and more business to "the Vehicle City." "Flint is wonderful, it is unique," Durant exclaimed. "In the history of the world, there was never anyplace like it and I am always glad to call it home. . . . Everybody is ready to help and work with everybody else for the good of Flint. . . ."[55]

As long as Durant focused on building the best cars for the lowest prices, General Motors grew and prospered. What he lacked in administrative and organizational skills, he made up for with his "intuitive flashes of brilliance" and his salesmanship. For many years, his work habits and integrity were legendary. He displayed the talent, perserverance, and savvy to run one of America's largest corporations. [56]

The problem was that General Motors began to receive less and less of Durant's time while the stock market on Wall Street captured more and more. The gambling bug bit him hard and a long talk with a broker was his favorite salve. He would postpone key decisions for GM and delay executive meetings while he studied Wall Street and gambled his millions. Walter Chrysler, the vice president in charge of all GM operations, could hardly ever get Durant's attention. "For several days in succession," Chrysler said later, "I waited at his office, but he was so busy he could not take the time to talk with me. It seemed to me he was trying to keep in communication with half the continent; eight or ten telephones were lined up on his desk. . . . 'Durant is buying' was a potent phrase in Wall Street then." In 1920, in the midst of such neglect of duty, Pierre duPont, chairman of the board, helped oust Durant and work out an arrangement to buy his GM stock.[57]

After this happened, Durant, as was his custom, went again to Flint friends to finance another project: Durant Motors Inc., which would feature the new Durant car. He also produced the "Star," which he showcased in New York and persuaded 231,000 people to plunk down cash deposits. His gambling fever, however, was sapping his energy and resources, and Durant Motors never made a serious challenge to Ford or GM. Instead, Durant formed a "bull consortium" of stock buyers who plunged into the stock market with billions of dollars. Durant himself had over one billion dollars in the market by 1928, which included accounts with at least fifteen brokers and phone bills of $20,000 a week. When the Great Depression hit, Durant's roller-coaster ride crashed. Durant Motors was liquidated; Durant himself declared bankruptcy in 1936.

Some of the entrepreneurial spirit, however, was still in him. Nearing eighty years of age, he opened a restaurant, hoping to make it into a national chain, and a bowling alley, hoping to do the same with it. The idea of building a chain business was, perhaps, ahead of its time, but Durant couldn't make it work during the 1940s. Durant died in 1947, the same year as Henry Ford, at age 85.[58]

What a remarkable blending William Crapo Durant was of his father and grandfather, the gambler and the entrepreneur. If Henry Crapo, 50 years after his death in 1869, could have returned to Michigan, he would have seen his "Willie," the entrepreneur, perched on high as president of General Motors, a grandson who took the family fortune and multiplied it beyond recognition. If William Clark Durant, 50 years after his death in 1883, could have returned to Michigan, he would have seen his son, the gambler, close down his car company and lose his fortune on the stock market.

The big winners were neither the Crapos nor the Durants, but the city of Flint and the state of Michigan. Michigan's old reputation as a frozen wasteland had been melted by the fires of industrial growth. The state's lumber resources, a precarious extractive industry, had been developed and diversified into carriages and then into cars. The talent to run these businesses came to Michigan and stayed there. Others who saw this happen would also be eager to come to Michigan, take risks in the state's alluring investment climate, and make it an industrial showcase for the nation, and even the world.

Herbert Dow as a young man.

4

Herbert Dow and the Liberation of the American Chemical Industry

"I CAN FIND A HUNDRED MEN TO TELL ME AN IDEA WON'T WORK," Herbert Dow once said. "What I want are men who will *make* it work."[1] When Dow fought to liberate the American chemical industry from a European stranglehold, he needed men to make his ideas work because almost everyone else told him he would fail. But from 1900 to 1930, Dow, more than any other American, helped oust the established Europeans from world leadership in basic chemicals from bromine to chlorine and in chemical products from aspirin to magnesium metal.

Born in 1866, Herbert Dow was a technical whiz and entrepreneur from the time of his childhood. His father, Joseph Dow, was a master mechanic and invented equipment for the U. S. Navy. He shared technical ideas with Herbert at the dinner table and the work bench in their home in Derby, Connecticut. He showed Herbert how to make a turbine and even how to modernize a pin factory. Whether Herbert was selling vegetables or taking an engine apart, his father was there to encourage him.[2]

As an adult, Herbert Dow would secure 107 patents for his inventions. But he developed his persistence and drive as a boy. Once it took him over forty tries to make and market a workable egg incubator, but he wouldn't quit until he had made and sold one profitably. And when that market dried up, he tried to sell copies of the blueprints. Find out what people wanted, Dow learned early, and then figure out how to give it to them cheaper than anyone else.

When Herbert was 12, he moved to Cleveland, where his father had become master mechanic for the Chisholm Shovel Works. Six years later, young Dow entered Cleveland's Case School of Applied Science. Case had a hands-on approach to learning and Dow flourished. He loved to take things apart and find out how they worked. Chemicals, and the manufacturing that made chemicals profitable, especially fascinated him.[3]

Dow's future as an inventive chemist was triggered during his senior year when he watched the drilling of an oil well outside of Cleveland. At the well site, he noticed that brine had come to the surface. The oozing brine was considered a nuisance by the oil men. One of the well-drillers took some brine to Dow and asked him to taste it. "Bitter, isn't it," the driller noted. "It certainly is," Dow added. "Now why would that brine be so bitter?" the driller asked. "I don't know," Dow said, "but I'd like to find out." He took a sample of the brine to his lab, tested it, and found lithium in the brine, which helped explain the bitterness, and also bromine. Bromine was used as a sedative and also in photography to develop film. This put Dow to wondering if bromine could be extracted profitably from the abundant brine in the Cleveland area. Others had extracted salt (sodium chloride) from the brine. Maybe Dow could do the same thing with bromine, and sell it commercially.[4]

The key to making bromine profitably was finding a way to separate it cheaply from brine. The traditional method was to heat a ton of brine, remove the crystallized salt, treat the rest with chemicals, salvage only two or three pounds of bromine, and dump the rest. Dow thought this method was expensive and inefficient. Why did the salt—which was often unmarketable—have to be removed? Was the use of heat—which was very expensive to apply—really necessary to separate the bromine? And why throw the rest of the brine away? Were there economical methods of removing the chlorine and magnesium also found in brine? The answers to these questions were important to Dow. The U. S. was ignoring or discarding an ocean of brine right beneath the earth's surface. If he could extract the chemicals in this brine, he could change America's industrial future.[5]

After graduation in 1888, Dow took a job as a chemistry professor at the Huron Street Hospital College in Cleveland. There, he had his own lab, an assistant, and time to work out the bromine problem. During the next year, he developed two processes—electrolysis and "blowing out." In electrolysis he used an electric current to help free bromine from the brine; in blowing out he used a steady flow of air through the solution to separate the bromine. Once Dow showed he could use his two methods to make small amounts of bromine, he assumed he could make large amounts and sell it all over the world.[6]

The next step for young Dow was to start the Canton Chemical Company. With grand thoughts but no experience, Dow persuaded three partners in Ohio to invest in his blowing-out process. The bad news was that his cheap ramshackle equipment turned out only small amounts of bromine. His company was cash poor and he went broke in less than a year. The good news was that Dow never saw failure as permanent, but only as a path to later success. He proved he could make bromine, and if he had a better source of brine he just knew he would thrive.

Before starting another business, Dow scoured the Ohio-Michigan area for brine with high bromine content. His journey ended in the small town of Midland, Michigan, 125 miles northwest of Detroit. After testing the brine in Midland, Dow approached J. H. Osborn and several Cleveland-area businessmen. If they would supply him with the starting capital he would use it to supply them with profits from the sale of his bromine. Together they launched the Midland Chemical Company in 1890.[7]

Again Dow struggled. He never had enough money because nothing ever worked as he expected it to. Electrolysis was new and untested. His brine cells were too small and the current he passed through the brine was too weak to free all the bromine. When he strengthened the current, he freed all the bromine, but some chlorine seeped in too. Instead of being frustrated, Dow would later go into the chlorine business as well. After all, people were making money selling chlorine as a disinfectant. So could Dow. Meanwhile, the chlorine and bromine were corroding his equipment and causing breakdowns. He needed better carbon electrodes, a larger generator, and loyal workers.[8]

Dow found himself working 18-hour days and sleeping at the factory. Sure, he was making bromine with his new methods, but it wasn't yet pure enough to market effectively. That made the Cleveland investors nervous and they balked at sending Dow more cash. He went weeks with delayed pay, or none at all. When unpaid co-workers wanted their cash, Dow had to promise bonuses and that led to more haggling with his investors.[9]

Dow had to economize to survive. He built his factory in Midland with cheap local pine and used nails sparingly. He saved 29 cents buying a padlock in Midland instead of Saginaw. "Crazy Dow" is what the Midland people called him when he rode his dilapidated bike into town to fetch supplies. Laughs, not dollars, were what most townsfolk contributed to his visionary plans. To survive Dow had to be administrator, laborer, and fund-raiser, too. He looked at his resources, envisioned the possible, and moved optimistically to achieve it.[10]

Dow needed three years before he could sell bromine at a profit. His investors finally cheered and relaxed, but Dow pondered and agonized at pouring all that unused brine down the sewer. If he could use electrolysis to separate the bromine, why not try to separate the chlorine as well? So while his investors moaned, Dow began making the wood and tar cells that would help him free chlorine from brine.[11]

Courtesy of the Post Street Archives

The brine well of Herbert Dow.

Dow's plunge into the chlorine business strained relations with his investors. But the final break came when his first experiment with chlorine blew up his building and destroyed his equipment. His investors were furious and demanded that Dow make bromine and forget the chlorine. This the persistent Dow refused to do—he left the Midland

Chemical Company and returned to Ohio. In the town of Navarre, he worked in privacy with a small staff trying to produce chlorine safely by electrolysis. New investors took notice of this, and some of the old ones also became interested.

In 1897, Dow returned to Midland and later organized the Dow Chemical Company, which would make chlorine bleach. Dow was the manager of this new company and he had raised $200,000 in new capital to run it. Soon he was using electrolysis to separate chlorine and his blowing-out method to produce bromine. By 1899, the new Dow company had absorbed the older Midland Chemical Company and Dow was ready to market his products throughout the country and even the world.[12]

For Dow Chemical to become a major corporation, it had to meet the European challenge. Germany, in particular, dominated world chemical markets in the 1800s. The Germans, and to a lesser extent the English, had experience and access to top-flight scientists and used them to monopolize world markets and control prices. The American chemical industry was almost nonexistent in the 1800s; whatever the Europeans charged, the Americans paid.

The Bleach War

Dow's first battle with the Europeans was in chlorine. Chlorine was traditionally used as a disinfectant, but its market as a bleach expanded in the 1890s. Newspapers were the reason. The inventing of the linotype machine and the rotary press created a new demand for wood pulp as paper. The dozens of new companies making wood pulp needed tons of bleach daily to change the pulp from wood-color to white. About forty companies throughout Great Britain began selling bleach to most of the world. They formed a cartel, or combine, called the United Alkali Company, which regulated the price and output of bleach throughout the world. The members of the United Alkali Company controlled the huge potash deposits in Britain, from which they made their bleach. They were so dominant that Dow could only sell competitively in the Great Lakes states, where lower shipping costs worked to his advantage.[13]

The optimistic Dow always believed he could match the United Alkali members in the price and quality of his bleach. What he didn't count on was the predatory price cutting they engaged in to knock Dow out of business. Here is how it worked. Each December, United Alkali announced a price for bleach for the following year. Before Dow entered the picture the standard price was $3.50 a hundredweight, a high figure that reflected United Alkali's near monopoly of the world market.

Just when Dow came on the scene in the mid-1890s, the British cut their price almost in half, from $3.50 to $1.87. But Dow had improved his efficiency enough to match that price. When the British saw this they cut the price again to $1.65. No one was fooled by these actions. As Dow later said,

> The reasoning that governed these prices is apparent; namely the United Alkali Company fixed the price in the United States at the highest figure they thought they could secure without bringing about competition. When they found competition was starting, they realized their American price ($3.50) was too high and they lowered it (to $1.87 and then to $1.65).[14]

Even after this last cut, Dow increased his bleach production from 9 to 72 tons per day from 1897 to 1902. His electrolysis method of producing chlorine was efficient enough to match the British price. Other American firms were selling bleach, too, and so the British went in for the kill. They decided to sell at a loss temporarily; this, they reasoned would oust the Americans from the market; then the British could hike prices later when Dow and the others were gone.

Late in 1902, the United Alkali Company announced another drop in bleach prices—from $1.65 to $1.25 (which included a 20-cent tariff, plus freight charges). The other American companies shut down and Dow must have been tempted to join them. But if he did he would lose not only a large part of his business, but also the chance to improve his manufacturing process as he increased his output. Dow believed he was the most efficient producer and besides, he hated giving in to a cartel.

When Dow agreed to match the British price, they slashed it again to $1.04. Dow barely survived during 1903, so the cartel announced it would sell bleach in 1904 for a large loss at only 88.5 cents a hundredweight. Dow countered by signing contracts for his entire 1904 output at 86 cents. That decision meant a $90,000 loss for his company. After he did this, the United Alkali Company cleverly announced it was raising bleach prices to $1.25.

Even so, Dow still honored his 86-cent contracts. This was hard to do because the company was teetering on the edge of bankruptcy. Even before United Alkali's last price cut, the company was $225,000 in debt and $92,000 overdrawn at a Cleveland bank. In fact, for Dow to get another loan to survive, each of the directors of the company had to endorse the notes. "It seems too bad," Dow wrote a stockholder, "that we have to bear the entire cost of bringing the United Alkali Company to its knees."[15] But by matching the low British price and honoring his contracts, he earned respect. The British gave up trying to oust Dow from the chlorine business and kept the price steady at $1.25.

The Bromine War

No sooner had the bleach war ended than Dow stumbled into a bromine war with Germany. In other words, his major chemicals—

chlorine and bromine—both were under strong attack in the early 1900s. The Germans had been the dominant supplier of bromine since it first was mass-marketed in the mid-1800s. The vast potash deposits in Stassfurt supplied bromine to the Germans as a by-product. Only the U. S. emerged as a competitor to Germany in the bromine market, and then only as a minor player. Some small firms along the Ohio River sold bromine, but only within the country.[16]

The reason the Americans did not compete with the Germans was because of force, not price. About thirty German firms combined to form a cartel, Die Deutsche Bromkonvention, which fixed the world price for bromine at a lucrative 49 cents a pound. Customers either paid the 49 cents or they went without. Dow and other American companies sold bromine inside the U. S. for 36 cents. The Bromkonvention made it clear that if the Americans tried to sell else-where, the Germans would flood the American market with cheap bromine and drive them all out of business. The Bromkonvention law was, "The U. S. for the U. S. and Germany for the world."[17]

Dow entered bromine production with these unwritten rules in effect. And he followed them for awhile. The bleach war, however, put him so deeply in debt that he decided to break the unwritten rules, challenge the Germans, and sell bromine in Europe to recover his losses.

Dow easily beat the cartel's 49 cent price and courageously sold America's first bromine in England. He hoped that the Germans, if they found out what he was doing, would ignore it. In fact, throughout 1904 he merrily bid on bromine contracts throughout the world.

After a few months of this, Dow encountered an angry visitor in his office from Germany—Hermann Jacobsohn of the Bromkonvention. Jacobsohn announced he had "positive evidence that [Dow] had exported bromides." "What of it?" Dow replied. "Don't you know that you can't sell bromides abroad?" Jacobsohn asked. "I know nothing of the kind," Dow retorted. Jacobsohn was indignant. He said that if Dow persisted, the Bromkonvention members would run him out of business whatever the cost. Then Jacobsohn left in a huff.[18]

Dow's philosophy of business differed sharply from that of the Germans. He was both a scientist and an entrepreneur. He wanted to learn how the chemical world worked; and then he wanted to make the best product at the lowest price. The Germans, by contrast, wanted to discover chemicals in order to monopolize them and extort high prices for their discoveries. Dow wanted to improve chemical products and find new combinations and new uses for chemicals. The Germans were content to invent them, divide markets among their cartel members, and sell abroad at high prices. Those like Dow who tried to compete with the cartel learned quickly what "predatory price cutting" meant. The Bromkonvention, like other German cartels, had a "yellow dog fund," which was money set aside to use to flood other countries with low cost chemicals to drive out competitors.[19]

Dow, however, was determined to compete with the Bromkonvention. He needed the sales and he believed his electrolysis produced bromine cheaper than the Germans could do. Also, Dow was stubborn and hated being bluffed by a bully. When Jacobsohn stormed out of his office, Dow continued to sell bromine to countries from England to Japan.

Before long, in early 1905, the Bromkonvention went on a rampage: It poured bromides into America at 15 cents a pound, well below its fixed price of 49 cents, and also below Dow's 36-cent price. Jacobsohn arranged a special meeting with Dow in St. Louis and demanded that he quit exporting bromides or else the Germans would flood the American market indefinitely. The Bromkonvention had the money and the backing of its government, Jacobsohn reminded Dow, and could long continue to sell in the U. S. below the cost of production. Dow was not intimidated; he was angry and told Jacobsohn he

Courtesy of the Post Street Archives

Wagonloads of bromine headed first by boat and then by wagon to Kobe, Japan, around 1905. It was such shipments to foreign countries that triggered Dow's bromine war with the Germans. Also pictured is the bromine plant with its wooden blowing-out tower protruding from the roof.

would sell to whomever would buy from him. Then Dow left the meeting with Jacobsohn screaming threats behind him. As Dow boarded the train from St. Louis he knew the future of his company—if it had a future—depended on how he handled the Germans.[20]

On that train, Dow worked out a daring strategy. First, he had his company sell a token amount of bromine in the U. S. at 12 cents a pound to persuade the Germans that he would fight them on their terms.

Second, Dow had his agent in New York discretely buy hundreds of thousands of pounds of German bromine at their 15-cent price. Third, Dow repackaged the German bromine and sold it in Europe—including Germany!—at 27 cents a pound. "When this 15-cent price was made over here," Dow said, "instead of meeting it, we pulled out of the American market altogether and used all our production to supply the foreign demand. This, as we afterward learned, was not what they anticipated we would do."[21]

On this last point, Dow secretly hired British and German agents to market his repackaged bromine in their countries. They had no trouble doing so because the Bromkonvention had left the world price above 30 cents a pound. The Germans were selling in the U. S. far below cost of production and they hoped to offset their U. S. losses with a high world price. Dow courageously repackaged and recycled their bromine and made money doing so. A. E. Convers, the worried president of Dow Chemical, backed Dow's plan. "It seems as though the only way to bring Jacobso[h]n to terms will be to demoralize his market if possible at the point where he is getting his profit."[22]

Meanwhile, the Germans were befuddled. They expected to run Dow out of business; and this they thought they were doing. But why was U. S. demand for bromine so high? And where was this flow of cheap bromine into Europe coming from? Was one of the Bromkonvention members cheating and selling bromine in Europe below the fixed price? The tension in the Bromkonvention was dramatic. According to Dow, "the German producers got into trouble among themselves as to who was to supply the goods for the American market, and the American agent [for the Germans] became embarrassed by reason of his inability to get goods that he had contracted to supply and asked us if we would take his [15-cent] contracts. This, of course, we refused to do."[23]

The confused Germans kept cutting U. S. prices—first to 12 cents and then to 10.5 cents a pound. Dow meanwhile kept buying cheap bromine and reselling it in Europe for 27 cents. These sales forced the Bromkonvention to drop its high world price to match Dow and that further depleted the Bromkonvention's resources. Dow, by contrast, improved his foreign sales force, often ran his bromine plants at top capacity, and gained business at the expense of the Bromkonvention and all other American producers, most of whom had shut down after the price cutting. Even when the Bromkonvention finally caught on to what Dow was doing, it wasn't sure how to respond. As Dow said, "We are absolute dictators of the situation." He also wrote, "One result of this fight has been to give us a standing all over the world. . . . We are . . . in a much stronger position than we ever were. . . ." He also added that "the profits are not so great" because his plants had trouble matching the new 27-cent world price. He needed to buy the cheap German bromides to stay ahead, and this was harder to do once the Germans discovered and exposed his repackaging scheme.[24]

The bromine war lasted four years (1904-08), when finally the Bromkonvention invited Dow to come to Germany and work out an agreement. Since they couldn't crush Dow, they decided to at least work out some deal where they could make some money again. The terms were as follows: The Germans agreed to quit selling bromine in the U. S.; Dow agreed to quit selling in Germany; and the rest of the world was open to free competition. The bromine war was over, but low-priced bromine was now a fact of life. While Dow was in Germany, he saw the bromine factories there and later the bleach plants in England. He concluded that his methods and factories for making both bromine and chlorine were the best in the world. "[W]e are therefore in a much stronger position than we ever were before," Dow concluded, "by reason of the Germans having respect for us, which is a very hard thing to obtain. . . ."[25]

Dow's Leadership

Dow talked tough, but he knew he had to improve to survive. He constantly worked at finding new products and new markets for his chlorine and bromine. One of the first uses for his bromine was in making mining salts for separating gold from inferior ores. These mining salts were a major Dow export and helped the gold rushes in Australia and

South Africa. He also expanded his bromine for pharmaceuticals and for photography. Dow won Eastman Kodak's business in the last year of the bromine war and personally serviced the large account the rest of his life.[26]

Chlorine was equally important to Dow. As early as 1900, he sold chlorine as sulfur chloride used to make rubber. When sales to rubber producers dropped, Dow used his sulfur chloride to make chloroform, which soon became an important Dow product. Another use of chlorine was to make carbon tetrachloride, which is nonflammable and therefore used in filling fire extinguishers.

Selling these new bromine and chlorine products was crucial; Dow early established his own sales department to push Dow products at home and abroad. The profits from these sales helped him survive the bleach and bromine wars.

Dow was a creator, but some of his innovations failed. He tried to use nearby Saginaw Valley coal to make dyes, but nothing came of his expensive tests. He also tried to use his mining salts to recover nickel from ore; but a more efficient method was discovered just when he had invested heavily in this idea.

When the nickel experiments faltered in 1908, Dow wrote, "It took my last dollar. . . . I did not even pay my tailor for clothes. . . . There has never been a time since I was married when I have been under the financial strain that I am at present."[27]

Dow's relations with his directors was sometimes cordial and sometimes strained. It was cordial when Dow was selling chemicals and earning profits. It was strained when he was challenging the powerful Germans or plowing capital into untested products. Dow supported expensive research and development before his standard product lines were profitable. The directors often disagreed. Dow typically would decide to risk the development of some new chemical compound and urge one of his scientists to conduct special experiments. Only then, with the experiments under way, would Dow tell the board what he had done. Angry outbursts and debate would then follow and Dow would usually win because the research results were tantalizing. Over time, however, more stockholders began to see that Dow was not only a superior chemist but also a brilliant entrepreneur. "He made us rich in spite of ourselves," one investor quipped. Finally, in 1918, Dow became president and chief officer of the company.

Dow's fertile mind was always thinking of new ways to get more chemicals out of Midland's brine and new ways to make these chemicals marketable. He promoted iron chloride for engraving work and zinc chloride as a soldering flux. Insecticides came next as the Dow product line expanded after the bromine war.

Jesse B. Fay, the company's patent lawyer and a major stockholder, helped Dow patent dozens of his discoveries and watched him turn a flow of chemicals into a mountain of cash. "So far as I am able to judge," Fay told Dow,

> your mind does not work according to any normal law. Logic seems superseded by inspiration. . . . Things that to the ordinary mind appear to be fixed facts and axioms, to you appear faulty and capable of being changed for the better in many ways. You start with one idea and before you can put it into words new avenues of thought open up to you that divert you from the original idea. . . . You should . . . not use up your energy in doing something that another man could do as well as you.[28]

Dow took Fay's advice and delegated authority whenever possible. One thing that helped was that he hired the best scientists he could find and turned them loose to innovate. W. R. Veazey, one of his top scientists, later recalled, "He encouraged everybody to find out things in their own way. It was not uncommon for him to put several people or a group of people to work on the same problem at the same time and run the whole show like a horse race to see which one would come up first with the answer."[29]

The better scientists imitated Dow's creativity. Charles Strosacker, for example, was often the opportunist, taking abandoned materials and making a marketable product from them. Mark Putnam was the perfectionist, who figured out how to make products as pure as possible. Ed Barstow was the innovator, who mixed and made new concoctions. Barstow worked out a way to treat chlorine with toluene to make benzoic acid, which could be converted into a popular preservative. Barstow also invented a complicated process that could separate calcium and magnesium from Michigan brine. That later allowed Dow to produce ammonia, Epsom salts, and calcium chloride, which was used for settling dust in mines and unpaved roads. When Dow pumped brine into his vats in Midland, more and more went into chemicals for market and less and less went into sewers as waste.[30]

Dow was a hands-on boss. Rarely was he in his office working. Usually he was in the labs talking shop or out on the floor giving advice. There was Dow, a shovel in hand, showing a man how to spread coal evenly over a fire. There was Dow, hands in the air, encouraging his chemists and arguing with them so vehemently that others all over the building could hear him. When problems were debated and resolved, however, Dow and his men were a united front.

Dow respected his employees, especially those loyal to him in the early and precarious years. In fact, one of the reasons Midlanders called him "Crazy Dow" was because he paid high local wages to get the best workers he could. Early in the company's history, Dow started a plan to share two percent of the company's profits with all employees each year. Dow knew this plan would make his workers more loyal and more eager to do their jobs well.

Money to Dow was a means to an end, not the end itself as it was to the German cartels. Dow once said, "I'd rather work for myself for

$3,000 a year than to work for someone else and make $10,000."[31] At Dow Chemical, he tried to create an environment where talented chemists would have satisfying lives helping Dow unlock the secrets of Michigan's brine and making cheap products from it to sell to the world.

The Dye Business

Dow believed he had to have the best chemists he could find if he were to catch up with the Germans. His triumph in the bromine war was only a start: Germans still dominated the world in most chemicals and would fight to stay on top.

The dye business, for example, was almost exclusively a German preserve in the early 1900s. Ever since synthetic dyes had been produced from coal tars in 1856, German chemists put energy, capital, and manpower into producing and nearly monopolizing the world's dyes. The German dye trust, like the Bromkonvention, shared secrets, fixed prices, and divided the world markets among its members. When rivals in other countries dared to compete, the dye trust cut prices and tried to knock them out of business. Those who bought dyes from rivals had to face an angry and vindictive dye trust—all of which helped keep prices high and the Germans on top.[32]

Even during the bromine war, however, Herbert Dow was planning to attack the German dye trust. He reasoned logically: Bromine was a major by-product of his brine; bromine was a key ingredient in the making of indigo; indigo was "the most important of all the dyes," the favorite of most textile makers, and the heart of German dominance. Therefore, Dow should hire organic chemists, give them space, and turn them loose to figure out how to make indigo and make it cheaply. When Dow tried to do this in 1906—in the middle of the bromine war—his directors flatly refused to risk the capital or irritate the powerful German dye trust.

In 1914, the outbreak of World War I reopened the dye issue. With Europe at war, England used its navy to try to starve the Germans into surrendering. That meant blockading German ports and that act was quickly felt in the United States. American textile manufacturers relied on the German dye trust; a blockade of Germany meant shortages, and shortages meant high prices for scarce dyes.

At one point, Germany tantalized its American customers by exporting dyes to Baltimore in submarines. Usually, however, the Germans artfully manipulated the dye shortages to coax the U. S. into pressuring England to lift its blockade. Count von Bernstorff, the German ambassador in Washington, cabled his leaders "that the stock of dyes in this country is so small that by a German embargo about 4,000,000 American workmen might be thrown out of employment."[33]

What a paradox this was. Before the war, the German dye trust threatened to ruin any American firm that bought any dye from Dow or anyone else. Now Germany, through its manipulations, forced American textile men to rush to Dow and urge him to figure out how to make dyes as quickly as possible. As prices skyrocketed, newspapers echoed the cry, "Why haven't our chemical companies experimented sufficiently to produce synthetic dyes, pharmaceutical products, essential oils, and synthetic perfumes, in the production of which Germany seems to have almost a monopoly?"[34]

As prices skyrocketed, pseudo-chemists throughout the country went to work trying to make yellow dyes out of banana peels and green dyes out of grass. Dow was more realistic. With prices high and the dye trust on the sidelines here was his chance to break into the indigo market.

In 1915, almost a year after Germany went to war, Dow made his move. He imported a top organic chemist from the University of Michigan, and then exhorted him and others on his staff to unlock the chemical secrets to synthesizing indigo. The investment he made in cash, equipment, and manpower shocked some of his directors—who found out only after the fact what Dow was doing. They were horrified and raised the following objections.

First, the Germans had taken many years of teamwork to figure out how to make indigo. Dow's team would have to produce this same indigo more quickly with fewer scientists and less capital. If they were too slow, the war would end (which, of course, could happen anytime) and Germany would quickly recapture lost markets.

Second, Dow, by betting the company's future on indigo, was bypassing the chance to invest in profitable but less complicated chemicals. Dr. Albert W. Smith, a chemist and a member of Dow's Board of Directors, found this point to be compelling. "The indigo proposition," he wrote Dow, "really seems the most difficult of many that might be tried. For that reason possibly the time and energy spent on that could be more profitably spent in making some of the other numerous organic chemicals that are very high-priced and whose manufacture would be decidedly simpler."[35]

Third, even if Dow's chemists could produce indigo in large and profitable quantities—which were two major assumptions—he would still have to fight the Germans after the war and maybe during the war for every indigo buyer in the world. Even Dow admitted this to be true. "It will require . . . a very large investment to complete an indigo plant," Dow told the Federal Trade Commission in 1915. "[T]he question will then arise as to whether the price will immediately be reduced the minute we start to manufacture."[36] Nobody doubted for a minute that the Germans would resume their customary price cutting in the dye industry, just as they had done with bromine ten years earlier.

With confidence and cunning, Dow believed he would discover how to make indigo and then sell it competitively with the Germans after the war. And that's just what he did. In December of 1916, eighteen months after Dow began his work on indigo, he shipped his first batch off to market at $1.50 a pound. At last, America was in the dye business to stay. When the Germans came back in the world market, Dow was ready for them. Through his own improvements, the price dropped to $.75 a pound after the war and $.14 a pound by 1925, which was less than the Germans had ever been able to charge. As Mark Putnam, a vice president at Dow, wrote years later, "This accomplishment, while important from an economic standpoint, was even more important from a moral standpoint because it tended to remove the heretofore strong doubts as to whether America could produce a self-contained and vigorous dye and organic chemical industry."[37]

World War I

Only four months after Dow began selling indigo, the United States entered the world war against Germany. With the U. S. desperate for chemicals, Dow became a major national figure and regularly traveled to Washington. The formidable Germans, with the best chemical industry in the world, were sending mustard gas and high-powered explosives onto the battlefields. But Dow was ready. He turned his scientists loose with confidence that he could whittle away at the Germans' advantages. As he told the Federal Trade Commission when the war began, "We have been up against the German government in competition, and we believe that we can compete with Germany in any product that is made in sufficient amount, provided we have the time and have learned the tricks of the trade. Until we learn the[m], however, we cannot compete."[38] During the war, Dow had been learning these tricks of the trade; without the threat of the Germans cutting prices and dumping surplus chemicals on the market, Dow's team had been freely experimenting with all kinds of chemicals.

Fighting the Germans on the battlefield must have struck Dow as being similar to fighting them in the marketplace. The plot was familiar: The Germans had a head start and they were using it to bombard their enemies. Dow had to somehow catch up and help give his country the weapons to fight back. He started with his building blocks— chlorine and bromine—and mixed, experimented, and rearranged them to make new chemical compounds.

With chlorine, Dow made chlorobenzol. Chlorobenzol was a major intermediate for phenol, which was used to make explosives, and aniline oil, which was used in making dyes. With bromine, Dow made tear gas, a valuable offensive weapon, and special bromides that would calm soldiers under stress.

Dow once remarked, "The . . . war was the equivalent of [an] infinite protective tariff and the chemical industries developed very rapidly. . . ." Without the risk of German dumping, Dow built more laboratories and bigger factories. He tried to make chemicals long dominated by the German cartels. Phenol, for example, had been a German import before the war, but during the war Dow produced over 23 million pounds of it for explosives. Another example is acetic anhydride, which was needed to varnish and strengthen airplane wings. Before the war, America bought all of its acetic anhydride from Germany. But during the war, Dow's team figured out how to make it and his company became the major American producer of this vital chemical.[39]

Dow's massive and effective war production helped the U. S. win the war and helped win the peace afterward. Many of the war chemicals Dow had made had peacetime uses as well. Phenol, for example, became a major ingredient in dozens of products from aspirin to plastics, and Dow helped make America a dominant producer of phenol after the war.

In another case, acetic anhydride, which Dow made to strengthen airplane wings, was also a key ingredient in making aspirin. Aspirin had been a German monopoly before the war and the Germans had charged $8.50 a pound for it. During the war, Dow began shifting some of his acetic anhydride into the making of aspirin for the soldiers. Afterward, Dow had his costs of producing aspirin down to 60 cents a pound; he was ready to supply America's needs and also to challenge the Germans for aspirin markets all over the world.

The novocaine story is yet another example of the Germans' inventing, then monopolizing, then overcharging, and finally collapsing. Novocaine was first synthesized by the Germans and sold as an anesthetic. They reaped monopoly profits and charged $1,600 a pound for novocaine before the war. But after the war, the defeated Germans had to turn many of their patents over to the Alien Property Custodian. Dow applied for the patent for novocaine, learned how to make it efficiently, and quickly slashed its price to $30 a pound. As a result, dentists and doctors around the world could use novocaine more freely to deaden pain.[40]

Dow's favorite new chemical from the war was magnesium. Magnesium, like bromine and chlorine, was one of the basic elements found in Michigan brine. Dow hated throwing it away and had tried since 1896 to produce it effectively and profitably. As a metal, magnesium was one-third lighter than aluminum and had strong potential for industrial use. When combined with other chemicals, magnesium was a chief ingredient in products from Epsom salts to fireworks to cement.[41]

Unfortunately for Dow, the Germans had magnesium deposits near New Stassfurt. So while he was struggling, the Germans succeeded in mining magnesium and using it as an alloy with other metals. In 1907, they formed the Chloromagnesium Syndikat, or the magnesium trust.

Even before the war, Dow began pouring more capital into magnesium, but only during the war did he begin selling his first small amounts of magnesium metal. After the war, Dow still could not match Germany's low costs of production, but he refused to give up. After his customary debates with his board, he plowed millions of dollars in developing magnesium as America's premier lightweight metal. Part of his problem was the high cost of extracting magnesium; the other problem was the fixation most businessmen had with using aluminum. Since Dow couldn't persuade aircraft entrepreneurs to use magnesium, he sold it to make wheelbarrows, automobile horns, and especially pistons. In fact, the winning car in the Indianapolis 500 race in 1921 used Dow's pistons; the publicity from that win helped showcase magnesium, but he needed to cut his costs further before he could sell to a large market.

The Germans had mixed feelings as they watched Dow struggle with magnesium. On one hand, they were glad to still have their large market share. On the other hand, they were nervous that Dow would soon discover a method to make magnesium more cheaply than they could. Their solution was not to work hard on improving their own efficiency, but to invite Dow to join them in their magnesium cartel and together fix prices for the world.

In a sense, of course, the Germans were paying Dow the strongest compliment possible by asking him to join them, not fight them. They had learned from long hard experience the problems competing with Dow. What's interesting, though, is that through the battles with bromine, indigo, phenol, aspirin, and novocaine, the Germans persisted in their strategy of using government-regulated cartels to fix prices and control markets. They continued to believe that monopolies were the best path to controlling markets and making profits.

Dow must have been flattered by the German offer, but he refused to join the magnesium trust. He had already shown the world that his company—by trying to make the best product at the lowest price—could often beat the large German cartels. "I am sure," Dow said, "that in the long run any artificial combination that restricts output or raises prices is ultimately detrimental for the consuming public, although it may be apparently beneficial for the immediate recipients of the extra profits. . . ." He called Germany a "finished country," one that clung to old ideas and shunned creative thinking. The cartels were part of an old imperial order, not the new democratic one where one respected customers and their desires for new products at low prices. He was probably not surprised when world competition almost destroyed the old Bromkonvention in 1927.[42]

The Iodine Cartel

Dow's last days were as creative as his earlier ones. He spent time playing with his grandchildren and experimenting in his garden. In 1930, the last year of his life, he was awarded the Perkin Medal, the nation's highest award in chemistry. Even in receiving this honor, he looked ahead to mining chemicals from the ocean and making an array of products for the next generation.

Dow's last major battle was not with the Germans, but with the British. The two chemicals at stake were bromine and iodine, and the issue involved was the supplying of usable gasoline for cars. The problem was that the low octane gasoline of the early 1900s caused engines in cars to "knock," which happened when the gasoline exploded unevenly in the cylinders. Scientists at General Motors had found that adding iodine to the gasoline eliminated the knock, but iodine was tightly controlled by a British-Chilean cartel. It charged $4.50 a pound, a prohibitive price that put Dow to work finding a substitute. His scientists, working with those at General Motors, produced ethylene dibromide, which, when added to tetraethyl lead, would stop the knock in engines. And it was about seven times cheaper than iodine. What was needed now was a cheap and plentiful source of bromine, which spurred Dow to mine bromine from the ocean by using his blowing-out technique to separate bromine from seawater.[43]

Mining bromine from the ocean was risky: Even if it could be done

Courtesy of Post Street Archives

An early photograph of the Dow family visiting the home of the Osbornes in California. Mr. J.H. Osborne was a good friend and an early investor. From left are Grace A. Dow, Ruth, Willard, and Helen. Herbert H. Dow is holding baby Osborne, who died at the age of three. Three children were to follow: Alden, Margaret, and Dorothy. Mrs. Osborne is standing in the rear. Willard became president of the company after Herbert's death and ran it successfully until 1949, when he was killed in a plane crash.

it might be too expensive. Dow, therefore, hedged his bets with a direct assault on the iodine cartel. One of his scientists, C. W. Jones, used Dow's blowing-out process to separate iodine from oil field brine in Louisiana. When Dow died suddenly in 1930, his successor and son Willard helped Jones build an iodine plant in McDade, Louisiana. In the next few years, Jones was able to produce iodine so cheaply that they broke the iodine cartel and slashed the world market price from $4.50 to 81 cents a pound. Dow now had two products—iodine and ethylene dibromide—that removed the knock from gasoline and this gave the company a solid stake in the booming auto industry.

Neither the British nor the Germans, with their cartels and their price-gouging, ever understood Herbert Dow. If they could have built a gigantic microscope over Midland, and studied him from day to day, they would have marveled at his openness to new ideas. Why did Dow like to argue so much with his men? Why not just fire them? Why did Dow patronize the only barber in Midland who told him to get his feet off the furniture? Why was he lying there in his orchard next to his grandson, riveted by the shapes of clouds? Curiosity and persistence Dow believed, not force and control, were the ways to unlock the secrets of life. His desire to reach large markets with cheap chemicals was a logical extension of his interest in people and his compulsion to figure out how things worked.

Will Kellogg is a testament to the adage, "It's never too late to follow your dreams." At the age of 46, he broke off from his brother to capitalize on the accidental invention of cornflakes. The small town of Battle Creek was lucky enough to witness his meteoric rise from a "flunkey" to a world-renowned entrepreneur.

5

Will Kellogg and the Cornflake Crusade

TODAY, KELLOGG'S CORNFLAKES ARE A STAPLE OF THE AMERICAN diet, but few people know the complex and often bizarre details of Will Kellogg's rise to fame and fortune. The making of the first flaked cereal is a tale of sibling rivalry, a new church, and a health-food craze all in the small town of Battle Creek, Michigan.[1]

Will Kellogg's story, and that of his family, begins with a strange man named William Miller, and his theology of Adventism. Miller, through a study of the book of Daniel, twice during the 1840s gave precise dates for the end of the world and the second coming of Jesus. His clique of true believers anxiously awaited these raptures, some in ascension robes and others in laundry baskets to carry them into the heavenlies. When the sun came up the morning after the second prediction, Miller was crushed. He gathered his band of disappointed followers and began searching the Bible for wisdom on how to live until Jesus did come. One thing that united all Adventists was the idea that Saturday, the seventh day of the week, not Sunday, was the true Sabbath. In 1860, they established their Seventh Day Adventist church in Battle Creek, Michigan, a western town in a state that welcomed evangelical religion.[2]

During the 1860s, leadership of the church passed to James and Ellen White. Sister White, as she was called, claimed to have had a vision from an angel who told her God's best way to healthful living. The instructions were clear: Avoid coffee, tea, tobacco, and meat; instead eat bread, fruit, vegetables, and lots of water. This dietary advice became part of the creed of the Seventh Day Adventists; they built the Western Reform Health Institute in Battle Creek to promote healthful living. There in Battle Creek, John Preston Kellogg, a broom-maker and Adventist follower, gave $500, the largest contribution, to support the building of the health institute.[3]

When Sister White began to think about operating the Western Reform Health Institute, she naturally looked to Mr. Kellogg and his family for help. His talented son, John Harvey Kellogg, sat next to Sister White in church and, as a teenager, began setting type and reading proofs for Adventist publications. Soon he was even writing for them. Sister White had another vision that John Harvey Kellogg was to be a leader in Adventist work. She groomed him for leadership in the health institute and helped pay his way to medical school.[4]

Young John Harvey, or J. H. as he was often called, was precocious and confident. He took a course on health at the Hygieo-Therapeutic College in New Jersey, and afterward attended what is now Eastern Michigan University in Ypsilanti. From there he received some of the best scientific training available in the 1870s at the University of Michigan and the Bellevue Hospital Medical College in New York City. He read the latest medical journals in French and German and became a master surgeon. When he returned to Battle Creek in 1876, he was well prepared to take over the Adventists' health institute and transform it into a first-class "University of Health."[5]

First, came a name change. Kellogg, ever the publicist, invented the word "sanitarium," a twist of the existing Latin word sanitorium. The small Adventist health institute became the Medical and Surgical Sanitarium. Nicknamed "the San," Kellogg promoted it as a combination hospital, spa, and boarding house "where people [would] learn to stay well."[6]

Kellogg pushed Sister White's recipe for good health: Avoid alcohol, tobacco, and meat. Drink lots of water. He added many of his own ideas, however: Count calories, avoid sugar, and get regular exercise. He called his health program "biologic living" and he put patients at the San through a daily regimen of calisthenics at 7:00 a.m., after which came cold-water baths, swimming, electro-shock therapy, and a vegetarian diet. The day would often climax on the roof of the San with J. H. leading the patients in a march for good health.[7]

Under J. H.'s confident and charismatic leadership, the San grew from a handful of patrons in 1876 to thousands each year by the early 1900s. Along the way, the San became the most popular and fashionable health resort in the country. Henry Ford, John D. Rockefeller, Jr., George Bernard Shaw, William Howard Taft, and Montgomery Ward, among others, came to the San to receive the latest advice in biologic living.[8]

J. H. knew that most Americans could not afford the visit to the San, so he wrote dozens of books to reach all the victims of poor diets. *Biologic Living* was a best-seller, and earned him a national reputation. *What Is the Matter With the American Stomach?* and *Tobaccoism: Or How Tobacco Kills* were among his other literary efforts. His *Itinerary of a Breakfast* was a challege to the fatty sausage and egg breakfast so popular among nineteenth-century Americans. To J. H., the path to human happiness went through the alimentary canal.[9]

Kellogg was at home whether he was lecturing to an audience of lay people at the San or discussing surgical techniques with the finest physicians in Europe. His books made him one of the best known physicians of his era, and his high degree of professionalism made him a respected member of the American College of Surgeons, the American Association for the Advancement of Science, the Royal Society of Medicine, and the American Medical Association. Dr. Charles Mayo, a founder of the Mayo Clinic, said he could recognize Kellogg's excellent surgery by the small neat scars he made.[10]

Not all of J. H.'s medical advice was sound. He condemned all spices, from mustard to salt. "Vinegar," he concluded, was "a poison, not a food." "Coffee cripples the liver," he insisted, and colas were "insidious poison." Nothing was more important than good eating, J. H. pronounced. To make his points, he often stunned listeners with overstatements. "If the whole truth were shown," he said, "it would appear that the causes of indigestion are responsible for more deaths than all other causes combined."[11]

J. H. craved the limelight and reveled in publicity. He always wore white and moved about with an entourage of secretaries, nurses, and hangers-on. Sometimes he dictated essays and books to his secretaries, who frantically scribbled for ten hours at a time. If he had to travel by train, he liked to call the station and demand that they wait until he arrived. There, several minutes late, before gawking passengers, the imperial and white-clad Kellogg would arrive with his retinue of secretaries and assistants.[12]

As the San grew in popularity, J. H. found that he needed a business manager. While J. H. was writing, lecturing, traveling, and showboating, he needed someone reliable to answer mail, fix meals, screen patients, and repair the building. Such a person would have to have J. H.'s full trust, but also would have to work for a small salary (first-year nurses, for example, were expected to work for mere room and board; the pleasure of studying under J. H. was sufficient pay). Any prospective manager would have to be competent but always subordinate to

J. H.: Strong egos needed not apply. In fact, no one applied. Instead, J. H. drafted his younger brother Will Keith, or W. K., as many called him.

J. H. was eight years older than Will and never let him forget it. When they were growing up, J. H. gave him whippings from time to time and also used his backside as a foot-warmer at night during Michigan's cold winters. Will was always shy and grew up in the shadow of J. H.'s stunning successes. Will could never match his older brother, and dropped out of school when he was 13. One teacher, he later wrote, "thought I was dim-witted." Apparently his family did, too. "My father," Will confessed, "was not insistent upon my attending school . . . regularly. . . ." So while J. H. was off at medical school mastering the techniques of surgery, Will stayed at home putting bristles in brooms. While J. H. read medical journals in French and German, Will peddled the brooms he made. "I was not an expert broommaker," he admitted, "but I preferred preparing the stock, ready for broommakers to use." Even with this he had problems. When Will's broom business in Kalamazoo failed, he returned to Battle Creek looking for opportunities—just about the time J. H. was looking for a lackey.[13]

Twenty-year-old Will became the perfect business manager for the San. His quiet bashfulness and rare smile offset his brother's flamboyance. At 5' 8" in height, slim, and balding, Will was a regular sight most summer mornings jogging behind J. H., who pedalled his bike around Battle Creek detailing for Will his daily chores. A self-styled "flunkey" and errand boy, Will worked 80 and sometimes 120 hours a week packing books, mailing invoices, serving patients, and balancing ledgers. From pricing products to fixing meals, he had dozens of duties. "I was always notified when insane patients succeeded in getting away," Will lamented, because he was the one who had to spend the night tracking them down. "I was so overloaded with work," he later wrote, "that I am conscious that very little, if any of it, was performed satisfactorily."[14]

Courtesy of the Kellogg Company

Will Kellogg as a humble broom salesman before signing on with his dictatorial brother, J. H. Kellogg.

Part of Will's crushing workload was inevitable. It wasn't easy keeping up with the energetic J. H., who started 30 companies and magazines in a 50-year span. Will was the one saddled with the details of making them profitable. What bothered Will more than the work was the atmosphere: He did the labor and J. H. reaped the glory. Will never had a title, and only grudgingly did J. H. give him an office and a top salary of $3 a day. "I did the work as business manager of the sanitarium," Will later wrote, "and got no glory and very little money. . . ." J. H. seemed to think it an honor to be his servant. Even Sister White and the Adventists eventually broke with J. H., partly because of his ego.[15]

Will was more a slave than an employee at the San. He had to call his brother "Dr. Kellogg." Reportedly, Will gave him a shave and shoeshine when needed. Once J. H. had a guest at the San, and he made Will stay up all night to escort the guest to the train station in the morning. Will wrote that "Puss [his wife] came up to the office about half past seven to see why I didn't come home. She was so scairt [sic] that she cried." No wonder his children rarely saw him and never really knew him. "Am afraid I will always be a poor man," Will confided in his diary.[16]

Indeed, Will might always have been "a poor man" had it not been for the accidental invention of flaked cereal. Fixing, preparing, and even inventing foods was always important to the San's mission. The task was challenging. Some regulars at the San so detested the bland vegetarian diet that they sneaked off to the nearby Red Onion, a "meat speakeasy" in Battle Creek, famous for its juicy steaks. A horrified J. H. tried to lure these patients back with a host of healthy alternatives to meat and sugar products. He invented peanut butter, for example, as a meat substitute. Other Kellogg creations were named Nuttolene, Protose, and Caramel Cereal Coffee.[17]

Will sometimes joined his brother in food experiments. This was the case during 1894 when the two brothers fixed a mass of wheat dough, boiled it for different lengths of time, and put it through rollers to press it into large sheets. They were merely trying to create something healthful and edible.

One night during these casual experiments, Will left the dough out overnight before he rolled it. When he later returned to the kitchen, he ran the dough through the rollers as before—but instead of forming a flat sheet, the dough broke up into flakes. Will was puzzled. The moisture had spread evenly to each individual wheat berry and the dough had broken into flakes instead of binding together. Will could have thrown the flakes out and mixed up another batch of dough. Instead, he took them to his brother and suggested serving them at the San for breakfast. J. H. wanted to crush them into bits, but Will prevailed and the flakes were served whole.[18]

The results seem to have surprised even Will: The folks at the San crunched happily during breakfast and asked for more. J. H. decided to patent the new process for flaked cereal. Meanwhile, Will also experimented with oat, barley, and cornflakes and served them regularly at the San. In fact, he had to start a small mail-order business to supply the wants of patients after they left the San. At 15 cents for each ten-ounce package Will was doing a brisk business—he sold 113,400 pounds of flakes in 1896, the first full year of outside sales. That was especially impressive because the Kelloggs only told former patients and Adventists about their product.[19]

"I confess," Will later said, that "at the time I little realized the extent to which the food business might develop in Battle Creek." Others did, however. Charles W. Post, a Texas businessman, came to the San to learn about biologic living and left with recipes for making cereal. He started a cereal company in Battle Creek mixing Kellogg ideas with some of his own. His success brought dozens of others to town and they made Battle Creek the cereal capital of the world. By the early 1900s, more than forty brands of flakes poured out of Battle Creek. They included Korn-Kinks, Corn-O-Plenty, Squirrel Brand Corn Flakes, Indian Corn Flakes, and even None-Such Brand Corn Flakes Toasted. Everyone in town, it seemed to Will, was trying to make a fortune from cereal except the Kelloggs.[20]

Will urged J. H. to market flaked cereal on a massive scale. Will firmly believed that selling breakfast flakes was a remarkable way to make money and peddle good health as well. J. H., however, thought the risks were too high.

"Let's be content with a small business," he told Will. J. H. also argued that such blatant commercialism might compromise his high standing in the medical community. In any case, he had already made his reputation. Why risk his fortune and his large house on a hazardous gamble with flaked cereals?[21]

Will had a tough choice: Should he stay with his brother and have security or should he take a risk and enter the flaked-cereal business? He ended up staying for several more years. The high risks and his lack of self-confidence still held him back. "I am myself lamentably ignorant . . ." he wrote his son. "The competition in the business world is such that the people with good educations are usually those who succeed." Besides, he was over forty years old. He resented his brother, but stayed with him anyway.[22]

Finally, J. H., with his high-handed management, helped push Will out of the nest. During one of J. H.'s foreign trips, Will experimented by adding sugar (technically "malt flavoring"), which was strictly forbidden at the San, to his flakes. Will also raised money and built a new food-processing plant to serve the growing number of customers who ordered the Kelloggs' cereals.

When J. H. came home he was furious. He condemned the use of sugar at the San and he ordered Will to pay for part of the new building out of his own pocket. At that point Will could take no more abuse. When the San burned down in 1902, Will told his brother he would help him rebuild it and then go out on his own. In 1906, at age 46, Will Kellogg would at last become his own boss.[23]

Once freed of his brother, Will looked at the positive side. He had years of experience in business. He knew how to balance books, run a company, make cereal, and sell it on a small scale. If thousands liked flaked cereal, why not millions? Will slowly and methodically began raising the $200,000 start-up money from former San patients. In 1906, with capital in hand, Will pursued his dream of changing the nation's breakfast habits. He became a cheerleader for flaked cereal, but he also had to be a diplomat. To secure J. H.'s reluctant cooperation Will had to give him a majority of stock in the new company. As profits came in, Will bought it back piece by piece, but for awhile he had to endure his brother's continued meddling. Nonetheless, Will's new freedom boosted his spirit. He wrote Arch Shaw, his business partner, "I sort of feel it in my bones that we are now preparing for a campaign on a food which will eventually prove to be the leading cereal of the United States, if not of the world."[24]

Such confidence and focus were needed to help him overcome early problems. Most people outside of Battle Creek were skeptical of flaked cereal and few grocers wanted to carry it. And even if they could be persuaded to do so, what kind of flakes should he send them? And how would he separate his product from the imitators on the market?

First, Will did some test-marketing and concluded that cornflakes were his most popular brand of cereal. He was too small to diversify; therefore, he would make only cornflakes.[25]

Second, Will decided to stake everything on advertising. It became the major item in his budget. Amazingly, his first ad began, "This announcement violates all the rules of good advertising." He couldn't ask readers to buy his product because most grocers didn't carry it. Instead, he gave coupons for free samples and then asked housewives to urge their grocers to stock Kellogg's cornflakes so that the coupons

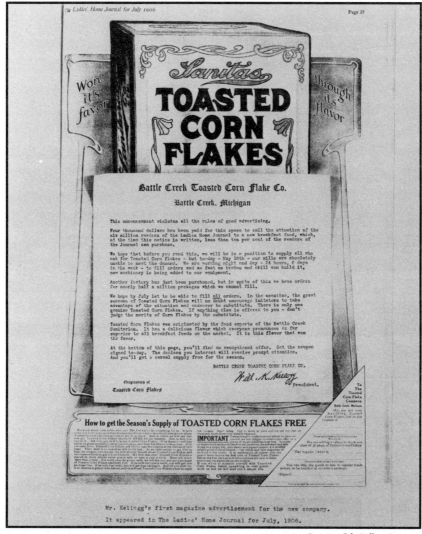

The Ladies' Home Journal for July 1906   Page 37

Sanitas
TOASTED CORN FLAKES

Won it's favor   through it's flavor

Battle Creek Toasted Corn Flake Co.
Battle Creek, Michigan

This announcement violates all the rules of good advertising.

Four thousand dollars has been paid for this space to call the attention of the six million readers of the Ladies Home Journal to a new breakfast food, which, at the time this notice is written, less than ten per cent of the readers of the Journal can purchase.

We hope that before you read this, we will be in a position to supply all who ask for Toasted Corn Flakes – but to-day – May 10th – our mills are absolutely unable to meet the demand. We are working night and day – 24 hours, 6 days in the week – to fill orders and as fast as brains and skill can build it, new machinery is being added to our equipment.

Another factory has just been purchased, but in spite of this we have orders for nearly half a million packages which we cannot fill.

We hope by July 1st to be able to fill all orders. In the meantime, the great success of Toasted Corn Flakes will no doubt encourage imitators to take advantage of the situation and endeavor to substitute. There is only one genuine Toasted Corn Flakes. If anything else is offered to you – don't judge the merits of Corn Flakes by the substitute.

Toasted Corn Flakes was originated by the food experts of the Battle Creek Sanitarium. It has a delicious flavor which everyone pronounces as far superior to all breakfast foods on the market. It is this flavor that won the favor.

At the bottom of this page, you'll find an exceptional offer. Get the coupon signed to-day. The dealers you interest will receive prompt attention. And you'll get a cereal supply free for the season.

BATTLE CREEK TOASTED CORN FLAKE CO.

Will K. Kellogg
President.

Originators of
Toasted Corn Flakes

To
The
Toasted
Corn Flake
Company

How to get the Season's Supply of TOASTED CORN FLAKES FREE

IMPORTANT

Mr. Kellogg's first magazine advertisement for the new company.
It appeared in The Ladies' Home Journal for July, 1906.

Will Kellogg's first magazine advertisement for the new company. It appeared in the July 1906 issue of *The Ladies' Home Journal*.

could be redeemed. These cornflakes, he promised, were nutritious and tasted great; they were more than just a health food. In October of 1906, he ran a similar ad in 17 magazines with over six million readers. All new ads carried this trademark sentence: "The original has this signature—W. K. Kellogg." Will was not vain; he just wanted to separate himself from his brother and his imitators. By the end of the first year, Will had shipped out almost 180,000 cases of cornflakes and grocers were lining up to carry his product.[26]

Skeptics told Will his cornflakes would never become a national product until he conquered the New York market. His response was a daring and risqué ad that read, "Wednesday is 'Wink Day' in New York." What this ad promised was that every housewife in New York who winked at her grocer on Wednesday would get a free box of Kellogg's Toasted Corn Flakes. Will first ran these astonishing wink ads in all major New York papers on Wednesday, June 5, 1907. "This advertising will arouse the curiosity of the entire city," Will predicted. And he was right. He sent posters to the grocers in New York to remind them that only Wednesday was Wink Day. "Don't give out samples before then. If anybody winks on Monday or Tuesday, tell them to wink on Wednesday." The Wink Day campaign quickly boosted Will's sales in New York from two train carloads a month to more than thirty.[27]

As Will soon learned, he needed more than good ideas to become the cornflake king. He had unexpected obstacles to overcome. For example, disaster struck just one month after he launched his remarkable "Wink Day" campaign. A raging fire destroyed his entire factory, equipment and all. There at the scene of the blaze, while some of his men were hysterical, Will was calm. "I want all you men to report here tomorrow morning," he told his employees. "You will not be laid off." The next day Will had a Chicago architect on the scene, planning a new fireproof building in a better location.[28]

Will used $64,000 in fire insurance money to help him rebuild. But the new factory cost more so he secured a promise of a $50,000 loan from a banker in Battle Creek. When the time came for Will to borrow the money, the banker reneged. "We're sorry," he said. "We're not

A hand-drawn picture of Will Kellogg working with a cereal roller.

making any more loans to food companies." For three weeks, Will desperately roamed the streets of Battle Creek and Chicago, seeking the loan that would keep him in business. Finally, a banker in Chicago looked at Will's ledger, judged his character, and said, "We have to take chances, same as other people." Will finally got his loan.[29]

The next obstacle came when Will ordered the water-cooled rolls needed in the new factory to make cornflakes. Unfortunately, only one manufacturer, a man in Detroit, made these rolls. One of Will's competitors, Charles W. Post, sensed an advantage and contracted for dozens of rolls, stockpiled them, and held tight to his monopoly. The Detroit supplier, meanwhile, had so much business under contract that he couldn't fill Will's orders for many months.[30]

Will later described how he went back to his old factory, walked among the rubble, and searched for inspiration. What good was a new building, skilled workers, and a great advertising campaign if he didn't have the cereal rolls to make cornflakes? Suddenly, he stumbled upon the old machinery—charred, broken, and useless there in the ashes. An idea came to him. He left quickly, called the Detroit rollmaker, and asked, "Does that contract of yours say anything against repairing broken machines. . . . You could get around the contract that way, couldn't you?" He then added, "We helped you get started in the cereal roll business. Now you've got to help us." The Detroit man sympathized with Kellogg and virtually made him new cereal rolls on the pretext that he was repairing the old ones. Post's monopoly was broken. Within five months of the fire Will was stronger than ever, supplying the winkers in New York and everyone else with all the cornflakes they could eat.[31]

Will's marketing genius, as much as the high quality of his product, helped him surpass the other cerealmakers in Battle Creek. Those who thought of Will as "J. H.'s flunkey" were startled by his success. He had always worked hard and he knew how to run the San, but where did this boldness, creativity, and confidence come from? Freed from his brother, Will showed entrepreneurial skills that few knew he had. A trained psychologist explained it this way:

> Dominated as he was by an older brother for many years, Will Kellogg developed . . . an inferiority complex. In overcompensating for this complex, Mr. Kellogg went to limitless bounds and it is likely this was the greatest driving force behind the success. He was going to show his brother, himself, and the world that he, too, had superior qualities and that only an unfortunate set of circumstances had prevented him from being as eminent as the Doctor.[32]

His boldness in advertising and his calm leadership during the fire were just the beginning. He promoted new products, such as Rice Krispies and All-Bran; his research team worked to improve the crunch

Following the successful launch of cornflakes, Will Kellogg promoted new cereals, such as Rice Krispies and All-Bran.

and the quality of his old products, such as cornflakes; and he improved his packaging and advertising to the point where Kellogg outdistanced all of his competitors. He changed breakfast habits around the nation and his name became a household word. His electric billboards lit up New York City; even Norman Rockwell later designed pictures for his cereal boxes. Cornflakes were munched the world over.[33]

Kellogg's meteoric rise caused many to watch him to see how he operated. "You sat in a meeting and if Mr. Kellogg was there . . . you seemed to feel the strength of the man," said one who worked with

Will Kellogg, a master marketer, built New York's biggest electric sign, which featured a mechanical device that changed the boy's face. He cries with the heading, "I want Kellogg's." He then smiles and the heading reads, "I got Kellogg's."

him. "[Y]ou sensed an interior reserve of strength, and this caused you to think that anything decided in that meeting when he was present was going to be achieved 100 percent. . . . [H]e had perfect self-confidence." Other people who watched Will in action said the same thing.

"He had determination and will power, bulwarked by an ability to go straight down the road," said a friend.[34]

Yet Will was never arrogant or boastful of his turned-around life. "I don't like applesauce," he said in reference to showing off. J. H. was Will's perfect model of how not to behave. Before and after his success, Will was quiet and avoided publicity. He refused to sit up front on stage, or to be honored publicly. "I don't care greatly to be seen of men," he said. If he had to attend a banquet he sat in the back, preferably in the last row. When some writer tried to do his biography, Will refused to cooperate. "I live in the present," he said. "Don't ask me questions about what has gone before."[35]

To produce the best product at the lowest price, Will needed to be frugal as well as creative. "This is wasteful," he would say and shut off a light or turn down the radiator in the factory. He kept his children on

Courtesy of the Kellogg Company

Will Kellogg in the cornflake factory, where he wouldn't hesitate to shut off an unnecessary light or turn down the radiator in order to minimize wasteful spending.

strict budgets and allowances. "I never had a taste for high living," Will admitted, though he did like to sneak a chocolate soda from time to time, and he also liked to travel abroad to improve his education.[36]

Will was frugal but not cheap. If he liked a new cereal or if he liked a particular advertising campaign he would back it to the hilt. He also paid above average wages and had high worker morale and few labor problems. Good wages for employees were important to Will because he was too shy to rally them in speeches or meetings. Even with officers of the company Will was reserved and formal. To Arch Shaw, his gregarious friend and business manager, Will confided, "I would give the world to be able to get along with people as well as you."[37]

Will may have been aloof from his workers, but in his own way he cared for them deeply. Even when he worked at the San, he often gave free meals and small cash gifts to people in need. Later, when he became a millionaire, he could help even more workers in their times of crisis. Sometimes he paid another's bill; other times he sent cash, food, or a load of coal. Unlike J. H., Will always preferred to give anonymously. He was embarrassed by effusive thanks and sometimes was harsh to protect himself from chiselers. Once during the Great Depression he sternly refused a plea for aid; after making his rebuke, he had his secretary send $200 in cash anonymously to the needy applicant.[38]

The Great Depression tested Will's ability to run a business and be a philanthropist. Above all, he wanted Kellogg's to be as strong as possible during the crisis. Selling cornflakes meant saving jobs and Will doubled the advertising budget to keep sales climbing. As the economy slumped, Will switched his factories to six-hour days to accommodate more workers. He focused on Battle Creek, too. When the Old Merchants' National Bank failed in 1933, Will arranged for his company, and three others in town, to accept only 40 percent of the money the bank owed them instead of the scheduled 65 percent. That move allowed the closed bank to give full refunds, not just 65 percent, to more than 21,000 other small depositors.[39]

When Will reached age 70 he began to think more about philanthropy and less about business. "I never desired to become extremely rich . . ." he confessed, but he had become one of the wealthiest and most famous men in America. During the 1930s, he plunked about $50 million, most of his fortune, into the W. K. Kellogg Foundation to coordinate and systematize his giving. Will knew that J. H. could never match that. As Will thought more about charity, he developed several ideas about how to give properly and effectively.[40]

First, he wanted his foundation to supervise his giving carefully to make the receivers accountable. "We will help people help themselves," Kellogg explained. He opposed the system of direct relief that the federal government began in 1932, in part, because it separated giver and receiver.

Second, he wanted to target special causes that he thought would help thousands and even millions if they succeeded. For example, he supported research for glaucoma and for restoring the hands of workers maimed in factory accidents. He also pushed farming research and even bought an 832-acre farm for Michigan State University to experiment with crop yields. Third, he wanted to create opportunities for children, regardless of their race or color. For example, he subsidized dental and medical help for children throughout Michigan. He also sank millions of dollars into improving rural schools and also colleges, mainly in Michigan. Will was often self-conscious of his own lack of education, especially next to his brother's, and he wanted to ease the path for others to stay in school.[41]

As Will rose from errand boy to cornflake king to world philanthropist, the one constant in his life was his rivalry with his brother.

J. H., who once called Will a "loafer" at the San, was disdainful and jealous of the meteoric rise of Kellogg's Cornflakes. J. H. pronounced himself to be the "real" Kellogg and he accused Will of selfishly exploiting the Kellogg name, which he, J. H., had made famous. Will bristled when he heard this. "For twenty-two and one-half years, I had absolutely lost all my individuality in you. I tried to see things through your eyes and do things as you would do them. You know in your heart whether or not I am a rascal."

J. H. responded by adapting the Kellogg name for cereals he sold at the San. The name Kellogg's Food Company replaced Sanitas Company, which allowed J. H. to compete more directly with his brother. Will countered in 1910 with a lawsuit: J. H. was infringing upon the brand name and consumers were confused. The Michigan courts decided in Will's favor and J. H. was restricted in using the Kellogg name to sell his foods. In defeat, J. H. waited for the chance to punish his upstart brother. In 1916, he took Will to court to bar him from selling bran products first developed at the San. But Will won this "battle of the bran," too, and left his brother with large lawyer fees.[42]

Will would need more than a couple of legal wins, however, to outshine his brother. J. H.'s dozens of books had sold over a million copies by the 1920s, and the San was a national landmark. J. H. added a glass-domed palm garden that displayed banana and rubber trees amidst the restful palms. In the main building, the massive columns, the walnut paneling, the crystal chandeliers, and the 265 rooms welcomed tens of thousands of guests during the 1920s. As usual, the San was the fashionable place for celebrities to see and be seen. Its clientele included politicians (Attorney General Harry Daugherty and Secretary of the Interior Gifford Pinchot), entrepreneurs (Henry Ford and Harvey Firestone), and writers (Upton Sinclair and C. W. Barron)—all fascinated by new health foods and the recipe for biologic living. Stewart

Courtesy of the State Archives of Michigan

J. H. Kellogg wrote a letter of apology to Will in the same year he died, but unbeknownst to him, his secretary never mailed it. He died without reconciling with his brother, but Will was finally shown the letter five years later, when he was near death.

Holbrook, who studied the impact of the San, concluded, "The influence of the Battle Creek Sanitarium on migration to Michigan has never been estimated but the instititution has perhaps attracted more visitors and possibly more permanent settlers—both Yankees and others—than did the Jackson, Lansing & Saginaw Railroad Company." [43]

The most magnetic celebrity at the San, of course, continued to be J. H. himself. Dressed in white clothes, with white goatee, and a cockatoo on his shoulder, he would show reporters how Johnny Weismuller, of Tarzan fame, broke a world's record in the San pool after dieting on San food. Or J. H. might be up in an airplane, courting photographers and discussing biologic living with Amelia Earhart. Occasionally J. H. would head off to Paris to study new advances in x-rays, or to Russia to advise Ivan Pavlov, the Nobel Prize winner, on the physiology of digestion. Much to Will's disgust, J. H. pronounced himself philanthropist extraordinaire, a benefactor to all mankind. [44]

Battle Creek was barely large enough to hold the two squabbling Kelloggs. The thousands who worked at the San or in the cereal factories knew better than to discuss one of the brothers in the presence of the other. After Will's wife died, he began to date and care deeply for Dr. Carrie Staines, a physician at the San. When J. H. found out, he threatened to fire her, which was proof to Will that he should marry her—and he did. [45]

The sibling rivalry came to a head in the late 1920s, when J. H. undertook a multimillion dollar expansion of the San. When the Great Depression hit, however, America's fashionable set stayed home and the San lost customers. Soon J. H. had to lay off workers to meet his payroll. While Will invested wisely and grew richer in the 1930s, the San went into receivership and had to be sold. As Will reached the peak of his career, he watched his brother relocate in a smaller building across the street. Ever the optimist, J. H. also opened a new health facility in Florida. At age 91, he did a photo shoot where he ran back and forth across a cinder path and then rode his bike in figure eights. "You've got to live right," he told them. "Feel that chest."[46]

Despite such bluster, the end was near for J. H. and he knew it. As he pondered his life and that of his brother's, he began to feel remorse. He had misjudged Will and he decided to make amends. In 1943, John Harvey Kellogg, possibly the most renowned physician in America, began to write a letter of apology to Will. So much of Will's life had been a reaction to his brother that the letter had to be done just right. "I earnestly desire to make amends for any wrong or injustice of any sort I have done to you . . .," J. H. stated. "I am sure that you were right as regards the food business. . . . Your better balanced judgment has doubtless saved you from a vast number of mistakes of the sort I have made and allowed you to achieve magnificent successes for which generations to come will owe you gratitude." There it was. J. H.'s recognition that his own star had almost faded, but that Will's would burn brightly for generations. J. H. closed his seven-page letter, gave it to his secretary to mail, and waited to see what Will would do.[47]

Will's response, however, would never come. J. H.'s secretary read the letter, felt it to be demeaning to her boss, and refused to mail it. That same year, J. H. died and the two brothers were never reconciled. Five years later, when Will was 88 years old and near death, the letter was shown to him. At last, at the end of a long career, he realized he had won his brother's respect and blessing. In those last years, Will was blind. He liked nothing better than to be driven to the Kellogg plant, park there, and listen to the noises from the factory—his factory. He had gone from uneducated "flunkey" to world-renowned entrepreneur. Even more remarkable, he had won his brother's blessing.[48]

Six photos of Henry Ford, whose astonishing victories in his early years were somewhat erased in the latter part of his life.

6

Henry Ford and the Triumph of the Auto Industry

I N THE 1920s, WHEN HENRY FORD BECAME THE RICHEST AND MOST famous man in America, he always made good copy for the pack of reporters who followed him around. When asked about the federal government, and the increasingly popular idea of centralizing more power in Washington, Ford, as usual, was swimming against the tide. "Our help does not come from Washington, but from ourselves," Ford said. "The Government is a servant and never should be anything but a servant."[1] With rugged individualism and brilliant entrepreneurship, Ford would live long enough to build a gigantic auto empire and, with a nudge from Washington, see it nearly collapse.

Ford was a national celebrity, but his life was steeped in Michigan history. His father William immigrated to Dearborn, Michigan, from Ireland in 1847, the year after the state sold the Michigan Central Railroad to private entrepreneurs. William Ford quickly became part

Courtesy of the State Archives of Michigan

A portrait of Mary Litogot Ford, Henry's mother. She realized early on that Henry was a "born mechanic." Henry, who came from a large family, had only one child, Edsel, with his wife, Clara Bryant. Edsel's son, Henry Ford II, ran the company for several decades after World War II.

of the team that rebuilt the Michigan Central and extended it from Kalamazoo to Lake Michigan by 1849. After his railroad days, he settled on a farm in Dearborn and married Mary Litogot O'Hern, an orphan who had been adopted by an Irish immigrant.[2]

In their marriage, Henry, born in 1863, was one of five surviving children; he talked often about the drudgery of the farm and his mother's love. Even before she died in childbirth, when Henry was 12, she called him "a born mechanic." According to Henry, his "toys were all tools" and he had a workshop before he had anything else. His early memories are often of machines: the first steam tractor he saw, a watch he was given, boilers, and sawmills. Henry's family cut much timber on their farm. If the lumber industry in Michigan had remained strong into the 1880s, Henry might have applied his mechanical skills in improving sawmill technology. Instead, after all the timber on his land had been cut, Henry moved to Detroit, with its factories and machine shops. He became a licensed machinist, had his first experience fixing internal combustion engines, and married Clara Bryant, who encouraged Henry's mechanical interests.[3]

After his marriage, Ford lived two lives: During the day he was a machinist for the Detroit Electric Company; at night he was mechanic extraordinaire, trying to build a motor car with a gas-powered internal combustion engine. Anyone strolling by the Ford house early in the morning of June 4, 1896, would have seen a strange sight: Henry Ford, ax in hand, was smashing open the brick wall on his rented garage. He had just started his first gas-powered car, and it was too big to fit through the door. Over the years, Ford would tell the story of this event over and over—the rain that night, the brief drive down Grand River Avenue to Washington Boulevard, and the seven years it took him to build his "quadricycle."[4]

What was remarkable, though, was not the event itself—others had already figured out how to build cars and make them run. What was most remarkable was that Ford grasped the implications of a horseless carriage and had the vision, perseverance, and ability to make cars for the multitudes of Americans. Many experts scoffed at the car; Woodrow Wilson called it the "new symbol of wealth's arrogance"; but Ford dreamed of improving its quality, cutting its price, and selling millions of them to average Americans all over the country.[5]

Courtesy of the State Archives of Michigan

Henry Ford in his first car, which he called a quadricycle. After seven years building his first car, Ford had to take an ax to his rented brick garage in order to fit it through the door.

Ford's path to building his car for the multitudes had many curves and hills, not to mention detours and dead ends. "No man of money even thought of it as a commercial possibility," Ford later wrote. This meant problems raising funds. His business manager, James Couzens, once said that Ford was thrown out of so many offices in Detroit that one time he just sat on the curb and wept. Even those who were making cars seemed only to want them for racing; and they always tried to get the highest price possible for each car. Ford raised the capital for two short-lived companies before he finally started Ford Motor Company in 1903. At last, Ford had the cash and the staff to churn out cars by the thousands.[6]

Ford was a hands-on boss and he hired others like him who were expert mechanics. Immigrants especially appealed to Ford. They were often excellent tinkerers, hard workers, and creative adapters. Charles Sorensen, from Denmark, went from pattern maker at $3.00 a day to production manager for the entire company. Carl Emde, from Germany, was a master toolmaker who helped Ford perfect the assembly line; James Couzens, from Canada, was business manager; P. E. Martin, a French Canadian, was plant manager in Dearborn; and William Knudsen, from Denmark, later helped Ford build branch assembly plants throughout the country. Ford cared little for titles and organizational charts. He would listen to and promote anyone who could help him produce his car for the multitudes.[7]

Right from the start, Ford insisted on quality. "When one of my cars breaks down," Ford wrote, "I am to blame." He searched throughout the world for the best materials he could find at the cheapest cost. Once he discovered the French were using vanadium steel—an exceptionally strong metal—in their racing cars. No American seemed to know how to make it, so Ford brought another immigrant to Michigan to build a steel mill and make some for him. "[T]hat is the kind of steel I want for the universal car I am going to build," Ford said. Shortly thereafter, he was using 20 different kinds of steel in his cars—one for strength, one for elasticity, another for durability, and so on.[8]

From 1903 to 1908, Ford made several different cars, including the Model N and Model K, but none satisfied him completely. Customers began to buy his product, however, and sales jumped from about 1,700 in 1904-05 to almost 8,500 in 1906-07. That gave Ford the cash to start buying out many of his partners. By 1906, he had a majority of the stock in Ford Motor Company, and that winter he began to lock himself in a back room to build his universal car: the Model T.[9]

After more than a year of tinkering, the Model T was ready to sell. It turned out to be the big breakthrough Ford was looking for. It was not luxurious, but it took people from one place to another and did so cheaply and safely. Most early cars cost at least $2,000, but Ford priced his first Model Ts at $850.[10]

The Model T became an American institution: It had a crank start, a flywheel magneto ignition, and a planetary transmission, which allowed it to rock back and forth. It had high clearance for bad roads, a four-cylinder engine, and vanadium steel in the crankshafts, axles, gears, and springs. And, at Ford's request, it was always painted black. It may not have been comfortable, but it was reliable and easy to fix. Ford established a network of dealers all over the nation and they had extra parts when needed.[11]

As more people decided to buy Model Ts, Ford got unexpected advertising from satisfied customers. One man drove the Model T down the Grand Canyon and then back out again. Another drove it to the top of Ben Nevis, a steep mountain in Scotland. Farmers discovered they could haul hay in a Model T; at least one farmer even used it to remove tree stumps. Finally, in 1909 the Model T won a publicized and hectic race from New York City to Seattle in just over 22 days—which was astounding given the bad or nonexistent roads and the mud.[12]

The versatile Model T also proved to be temperamental. According to Garet Garrett,

> It was a mechanical animal such as never existed before and will never be seen again. . . . It had some of the characteristics of a mule, the patience of a camel, the courage of a bull

terrier, and in bad situations it could be very gallant, although there was latent in it a whimsical hostility to the human race. When you cranked it on a cold morning it might come at you.

Some called their Model Ts "Tin Lizzies"; others, with a pompous streak, preferred "Phourde" or "IV D."[13]

With sales on the rise, Ford did something daring: He further slashed the price of a Model T—sometimes so steeply that he risked taking losses. "Our policy is to reduce the price, extend the operations, and improve the article," Ford wrote. "You will notice the reduction of price comes first." He explained, "We have never considered any costs as fixed. Therefore, we first reduce the price to a point where we believe more sales will result." The first Model Ts in 1908-09 sold for $850; by 1912-13, Ford knocked the price down to $600 and sales leaped from about 18,000 to 168,000. "Every time I reduce the charge for our car by one dollar, I get a thousand new buyers," Ford rejoiced. Meanwhile, he kept improving his product: "We will rip out anything once we discover a better way," he promised.[14]

One of these better ways was his development of assembly-line production. He didn't invent the assembly line, but he adapted it perfectly to car production.

When Ford was selling only ten cars a day he would have skilled mechanics completing most of each car individually from start to finish. As sales surged to almost 1,000 per day that system became impossible. Ford and his staff decided to freeze the design of the Model T. Then they broke down the making of a car into dozens of small tasks. Each worker specialized in one of these tasks, such as attaching the engine to the frame or putting on the steering wheel. Workers stood next to each other beside a long moving conveyor belt and did their specialized tasks until, one by one, completed Model Ts came off the belt every thirty seconds.[15]

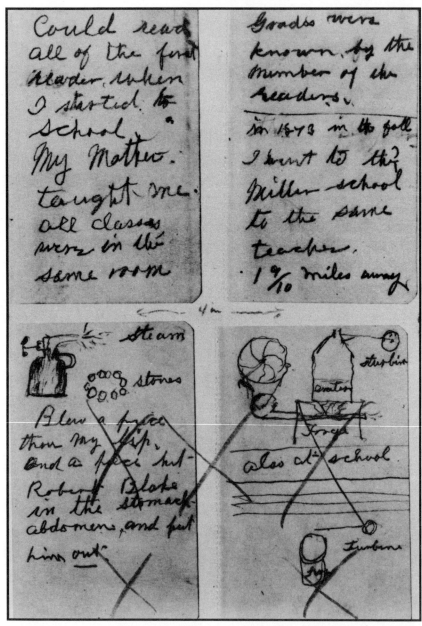

Courtesy of the State Archives of Michigan

Henry Ford, who was known to say "history is bunk," kept a notebook of life's events and built Greenfield Village, which he stocked with old equipment, buildings, and houses, including his boyhood home in Dearborn.

The assembly line slashed the amount of time needed to complete each car from about 12.5 to 1.5 hours. That meant Ford could meet the crushing demand for orders for Model Ts—sales were about 78,000 in 1911-12 before the assembly line and more than 248,000 in 1913-14 after the assembly line was fully put in place. Naturally, Ford cut the price during this time from $690 to $550, which made it affordable to another layer of middle-class Americans.[16]

One argument against the assembly line was that it was monotonous work. Ford almost conceded this point when he said, "There is not much personal contact—the men do their work and go home. . . ." Ford did keep his factories well lighted and ventilated; and he worked hard to prevent accidents on the job. But the work was not too challenging. Partly as a result, he (and many other industrial employers) had high rates of turnover and absenteeism. Ford found himself spending $100 to train each new worker, but many of these men only stayed for a month or two and then quit.[17]

Ford's reaction to this was dramatic: In 1914, he doubled his minimum wage to five dollars per day and he cut daily working hours from nine to eight. Such an experiment caught the industrial world by surprise. His competitors were startled; his workers were energized; and Ford himself was ecstatic. Some of the most talented workers in Detroit lined up by the thousands to apply for jobs with Ford. He couldn't hire as many as he would have liked because turnover and absenteeism almost disappeared overnight. No one wanted to lose his job. As a result, production surged and profits skyrocketed. Ford happily paid the higher wages and also cut the price of the Model T over 10 percent in 1914, 1915, and again in 1916. With each cut, more and more of his workers could afford to buy the cars they were making.[18]

Ford was delighted to violate "the custom of paying a man the smallest amount he would take." And yet "[t]here was . . . no charity in any way involved. . . . The payment of five dollars a day for an eight-hour day was one of the finest cost-cutting moves we ever made. . . ." So pleased was Ford that in 1922, when Model T sales began to top the million-a-year level, that he raised his minimum wage to six dollars a day. Meanwhile, he cut the price of Model Ts to about $300 each. With all of their manufactured steel, vulcanized rubber, and processed plate glass, Model Ts were selling at about 25 cents a pound—perhaps the best bargain in the industrialized world.[19]

Ford was paternalistic. He wanted his business to promote strong families and high moral character. Therefore, he reserved the right to check on his workers and make sure they were not wasting their doubled wages on whiskey and wild women. If they were, Ford would sometimes fire them and give someone else the chance to make five dollars a day. Historians have often criticized Ford for his character tests, but few firings occurred and morale on the assembly line in the 1910s and even into the 1920s was usually very high.[20]

The sales of Model Ts passed one million in 1920, and peaked at almost 1.8 million in 1923. At that time, well over half the cars on the roads were Model Ts, and Ford had become a billionaire. Not only did Ford "put America on wheels," he changed the way businessmen priced their products and paid their workers. He had helped centralize the auto industry in Michigan and secured that state's place in the nation's industrial future. He was an American folk hero and a national celebrity. The mere presence of Henry Ford in a barber shop getting a shave was an excuse for scores of locals to peek in the shop, noses pinched to the glass to get a good look at this man who had changed their world so profoundly.[21]

Much about Ford endeared him to Americans. He was a son of the soil, a near Horatio Alger story, and a doer not a talker. Once, in fact, when he had to speak to the prisoners in Sing Sing he said only two sentences: "Boys, I'm glad to see you here. I've never made a speech in my life and never expect to." The rustic Ford refused to socialize with the Detroit social elite. Instead, he liked to square dance with his wife Clara and listen to old-time fiddlers. He said, "History is bunk," but he made it and wanted to preserve it, too. He built Greenfield Village and stocked it with old equipment, buildings, and houses, including his boyhood home.[22]

Ford liked people who worked hard and made things, not bankers and lawyers, who he thought lived off the work of others. Even his dislike of Jews reflected more their reputation as bankers than their theology. He was equally at home with an immigrant mechanic as he was with his friend, Thomas Edison. He loved a good practical joke and would sometimes surprise friends by kicking them in their rear ends. Ford and Edison, in fact, once had a kicking match in the lunchroom of a posh New York hotel and they broke one chandelier and whacked another.[23]

Ford was not a church-goer, but he promoted thrift, hard work, and temperance. His eating habits became comical, in part because he listened to J.H. Kellogg. Ford liked vegetarian life and thought carrots were the perfect food. He wouldn't eat chickens because they ate bugs; he refused to eat sugar because he thought the crystals would cut open his stomach. Sometimes he ate weed sandwiches; other times soybean burgers. Guests of Ford often found themselves served that which they knew not, and wished they had eaten not.[24]

Above all, Ford was a man of action. When he saw something wrong, he wanted to do something about it, whether fixing an engine or saving the Europeans from World War I. If experts told him he couldn't do something, he worked at it anyway and usually succeeded. "There wouldn't be any fun for us if we didn't try things people say we can't do," he teased.[25]

For example, Ford wanted to produce plate glass in a continuous big ribbon, but the experts he asked all told him exactly why this was impossible. When they left, Ford took men who had never been in a

Courtesy of the State Archives of Michigan

Henry Ford owed much to the bicycle, with its wheels, gears, axles, tires, and frame, for inspiring his vision of a car.

glass factory and told them if they worked at it he knew they could make a continuous ribbon of plate glass—and they did. And now every carmaker does. "Our new operations are always directed by men who have no previous knowledge of the subject and therefore have not had a chance to get on really familiar terms with the impossible," Ford explained.[26]

Ford knew almost nothing about politics, but he was so famous that politicians couldn't resist trying to enlist his help. President Woodrow

Wilson persuaded the Republican Ford to run for U. S. Senate in Michigan in 1918 as a Democrat. He did so and would have won even without campaigning if the Republican candidate, Truman Newberry, had not broken so many election laws. After an investigation, Newberry was forced to resign from office. In 1924, reporters and admirers almost stirred Ford into running for president, but the campaign was nixed when Clara said, "If Mr. Ford wants to go to Washington, he can go, but I'll go to England."[27]

In political philosophy, Ford was not consistently laissez-faire, but he usually was because of his strong individualism. He argued that private enterprise was the way to solve problems in America. "The welfare of the country is squarely up to us as individuals. That is where it should be and that is where it is safest. Governments can promise something for nothing but they cannot deliver." Ford himself, by contrast, was delivering tens of thousands of jobs, all with good wages and only eight-hour days.[28]

Those people often shunned as second-class citizens were doing well with Ford. Blacks found the color barrier easier to cross at Ford and they were hired there by the thousands. Ford also hired handicapped persons whenever he could—including bedridden patients who happily screwed nuts and bolts together in mini-assembly lines in their rooms. Ex-convicts often found themselves with clean slates at the Ford Motor Company. Ford wanted to give every man a chance. Once, when driving to work, he saw a vagrant on the road. Ford eagerly picked him up and gave him a job in the factory. In this case, the man quit after six weeks, but Ford was at least content that he had given the man a chance.[29]

Ford relished the opportunity to compete for buyers in an open market. All he wanted was the freedom to operate as he thought best—whom to hire, what to pay, what kind of cars to make, and how much to charge for them. Ford expected to rise or fall on the basis of his decisions in these areas. He rose to the top because he made wise choices. The railroad industry, by contrast, frustrated Ford because it became strongly regulated by the Interstate Commerce Commission in the early 1900s. Ford decided to buy the Detroit, Toledo, and Ironton Railroad to bring supplies to his factories at Highland Park and River Rouge. In Ford's words, he tried to "reduce our rates and get more business. We made some cuts, but the Interstate Commerce Commission refused to allow them! Under such conditions why discuss the railroads as a business?" Ford would just make cars, instead.[30]

The early car industry had no such federal regulations, but it did have monopolists who wanted to use government to stifle competition. George Selden, for example, received a U. S. patent in 1879 for a gas-powered internal combustion engine. Although Selden never

Courtesy of the State Archives of Michigan

Henry Ford sitting on a tractor.

made or sold any cars, he argued that those who later did so were violating his patent rights. He sued for royalties and the lower courts upheld his patent. American carmakers formed the Association of Licensed Automobile Manufacturers (A. L. A. M.) and paid Selden royalties of 1.5 percent per car, and also regulated who would be allowed to make cars and who wouldn't. All American auto makers except one were in the A. L. A. M. Always the individualist, Ford refused to join the A. L. A. M., refused to pay them license fees, and refused to let them tell him how to make his cars. He went to court and argued that Selden's patent did not cover the modern internal combustion engines that he was using. After long litigation, the courts eventually agreed with Ford. The monopoly was broken in 1910.[31]

After the Selden patent decision, Ford and the other automakers just naturally looked to market forces to solve their business problems. The building of roads and highways, for example, was urgent with the growing number of car drivers on the streets. Car taxes were only a small source of revenue for road building, so Ford made gifts of land and money to build roads in Michigan. Other private groups built highways. They raised millions of dollars from those who had the most to gain from good roads: car manufacturers, tire makers, and cement producers, among others. The Dixie Highway, from Detroit to Florida, and the Lincoln Highway, from Indianapolis to San Francisco, are examples of highways largely built and operated by private groups.[32]

Ford argued that private enterprise was the best way to attack poverty on the national level. "Poverty can be done away with only by plenty," Ford argued, and he looked to "the day when production and distribution will be so scientific that all may have according to ability and industry." For example, Ford wanted to increase prosperity in the South; he argued that waterpower along the Tennessee River was a key source of economic development there. During World War I, the government had partly completed the Wilson Dam at Muscle Shoals,

Alabama. Two nitrate plants and a quarry were also built nearby. Some observers wanted the government to finish the project, but Ford stepped in during the early 1920s and offered to do the job himself. He made a complicated bid of about $10 million for the incomplete dam and deteriorating plants at Muscle Shoals. Interest groups and politicians all over the South supported Ford's bid and his vision of factories and small towns dotting the Tennessee Valley. Congress, however, refused to accept Ford's bid and turned the project over to the government (the Tennessee Valley Authority) in the 1930s.[33]

Courtesy of State Archives of Michigan
Henry Ford (center) pictured with Thomas Edison (right) and Harvey Firestone (left). Edison and Ford were frequent travel companions, joined occasionally by Firestone.

Henry Ford seems to have reached his peak as an entrepreneur sometime in the early to mid-1920s. If he had died in, say, 1925, at age 62, many would have ranked him with George Washington and Abraham Lincoln as a hero of American history. Instead, Ford lived on till 1947, and in his last two decades he badly damaged his heroic reputation.

He seems to have suffered a gradual mental decline; his thinking, usually so flexible and creative, became rigid and unimaginative. He also became mean to those around him who disagreed with his taste in cars, art, food, or almost anything else. During these years, his good labor relations crumbled. The man who gave the nation the five-dollar day with the forty-hour week later adopted the speed up and the stretch out on the assembly line. Ford still had his moments of triumph—building the Model A and inventing the V-8 engine, for example—but more often he stumbled into adversity.[34]

An early symptom of Ford's decline was his refusal to improve the Model T. By the early 1920s, his son Edsel and others in the company urged him either to change the Model T or produce a more modern car. Ford not only refused, he fired or shamed those who criticized the Model T. The "Ford Alumni Association" was the name given to the growing number of talented executives who were fired or who quit the company. "It is strange," Ford wrote in 1922, "how just as soon as an article becomes successful, somebody starts to think that it would be more successful if only it were different. There is a tendency to keep monkeying with styles and to spoil a good thing by changing it."[35]

What Ford was ignoring here were the changes in auto technology that had been made after he froze the design of the Model T. By the early 1920s, for example, General Motors cars had automatic starters, hydraulic brakes, and balloon tires. William Knudsen left Ford for General Motors and under his leadership the Chevrolet began to challenge the Model T. Even with sales slipping, Ford refused to change. His Model T still appealed to the purse, but not so much to the eye, ear, or back. The new Chevrolets were more stylish, less noisy, and more comfortable to ride in. As a Chicago woman wrote Ford, "My bones will not talk agreeably to one another" after a long drive in a

Model T. What's more, by 1924, the new Chevrolet had a water-pump cooling system, an oil gauge on the dash, a reliable ignition system, a foot accelerator, and a gas tank in the rear for safety and convenience. And the new Chevys came in all colors. The era of Ford dominance was over.[36]

In 1927, shortly after the fifteen millionth Model T rolled off the assembly line, Henry Ford could no longer ignore the complaints from his dealers and the slump in sales. His response, however, startled everyone: He abruptly shut down his factories, laid off his workers, and went to work on a new car. For the next 18 months, Ford and his staff crafted his next creation—the Model A. The new car was exquisitely made and sold 1.7 million in 1929—which partly vindicates Ford's entrepreneurship. One of his problems, however, was that General Motors was changing models each year to incorporate new technology and cater to fashions in style. Ford's strategy of manufacturing a good car, putting it on the assembly line, and selling it almost unchanged for 15 years no longer appealed to American consumers. Ford, however, was stubborn and slow to change his ways. The sales of the Model A dropped steadily during the early 1930s and Ford fell permanently behind General Motors in car sales. Even his development of the powerful V-8 engine in 1932 did not win him back most of his old customers.[37]

What is especially revealing here is that Ford, by 1927, was willing to lay off most of his workers in Michigan and abandon all of his dealers throughout the country. Most people want security in a job because they need to work to support their families. Ford, being a great risk-taker, did not see clearly why so many of his employees valued security in their jobs so highly. He seemed to expect them to fend for themselves until he figured out how to make a new car. Many good workers and dealers left Ford Motor Company forever; and those who came back later were wiser about the insecurity of their jobs with Ford.[38]

The Great Depression, which hit the United States with full force in the 1930s, was a major blow to Ford. The car industry had become the largest in the country in dollar value; other industries, from highway construction to machine tools, also depended on the autos. When vehicle sales dropped from 5.3 million in 1929 to 1.8 million in 1933, the whole American economy suffered. Ford, General Motors, and Chrysler laid off tens of thousands of workers at a time. The whole Detroit area became an unemployment zone.[39]

Neither Ford nor anyone else at the time seemed to understand what caused the Great Depression, or how to get out of it. Even today, the experts disagree.

This point is important because most of Ford's problems in the 1930s stemmed from this economic collapse that he did nothing to create and everything to avoid. The stock market crash of October 1929 clearly triggered a negative chain reaction of bank failures and business disasters. Much more, however, was involved and government was often the culprit. The highly restrictive Smoot-Hawley Tariff of 1930, for example, angered Europeans and they boycotted American cars. What's more, England, France, and other countries refused to repay the U. S. almost $10 billion in loans from World War I. Among other problems, the Federal Reserve raised interest rates in the early 1930s, and this made it hard for businesses to borrow money to expand.[40]

Ford's natural optimism and confidence in the American economy made him seem foolish in the 1930s. After a violent hunger march in Detroit in 1932, Ford said, "If we could only realize it, these are the best times we have ever had." The previous year he had called the Depression, "a wholesome thing in general." Such talk discredited Ford's free-market solutions and encouraged many in Michigan and elsewhere to turn to government for help—a move that would change Ford Motor Company forever.[41]

The major push for a planned economy came from President Franklin Roosevelt after his election in 1932. Early in his first term, he launched a vast program of government intervention in the economy. One of his proposals was to cartelize American industry along the lines of the German chemical industry of the early 1900s. The National Industrial Recovery Act (NIRA), passed in 1933, set up the National Recovery Administration (NRA). The NRA required American business to regulate itself through signed codes of behavior that would legally bind all companies within an industry. Competition would be almost completely eliminated. Under most codes, the industries would set production quotas, prices, wages, and work hours. The law also gave labor the right to organize and collectively bargain. As Ford said on the day the NRA became law, the government "has not any too rosy a record in running itself this far."[42]

As American industrialists rushed to Washington to comply with the NRA, Ford resisted and refused to sign any code. "I do not think that this country is ready to be treated like Russia for a while," Ford wrote in his notebook. "There is a lot of the pioneer spirit here yet." However, General Motors, Chrysler, and the smaller independents eagerly signed Blue Eagle codes that, under penalty of fine and imprisonment, regulated their production, wages, prices, and hours of work. Ford was astounded: His colleagues preferred stability and government regulation to competition and free trade. He was especially irritated when Pierre S. duPont, the former head of General Motors, urged him at a party to sign the code.[43]

As journalist Garet Garrett has written, "But for the Ford Motor Company, it would have to be written that the surrender of American businesss to government [the NRA] was unanimous, complete, and unconditional." Ford stood almost alone, defying the law, and pronouncing it un-American and unconsititutional. He needed a legal loophole to keep out of jail and his lawyers found him one: He didn't need to sign the auto code, he now argued, as long as he complied with its provisions. This he did with good humor. "The code minimum wage is hardly a good dole," Ford teased. Later he said of the auto code, "If we tried to live up to it we would have to live down to it." No government bureaucrats would leaf through his books and tell him how to run his business.[44]

Hugh Johnson, the NRA chief, and President Roosevelt, however, wanted government control as well as compliance. They tried to pressure Ford into signing the code, and when he refused they tried force. Ford would receive no government contracts until he signed—and with the large increase in government agencies during the 1930s, that meant a huge business. For example, the bid of a Ford agency on 500 trucks for the Civilian Conservation Corps was $169,000 below the next best offer. The government announced, however, that it would reject Ford's bid and pay $169,000 more for the trucks because Ford refused to sign the auto code. Finally, in May 1935, the Supreme Court struck down the NRA and Ford was allowed to compete again for any car business he wanted to.[45]

Ford had little time to celebrate—he spent much of the rest of 1935 and 1936 trying to escape the tax man. President Roosevelt's New Deal had almost doubled the national budget and somebody had to pay for the new government programs for farmers, businessmen, veterans, silver miners, youth, the unemployed, and many others. First, Roosevelt hiked the income tax on the rich to a marginal rate of 79 percent (later 91 percent). Second, he supported the first federal taxes on cars, tires, and gasoline. Third, he promoted the Wealth Tax of 1935, which instituted an inheritance tax of 70 percent on large estates. The first of these taxes was hard on Ford; the second was hard on all car owners; the third made it impossible for Ford to give his company to Edsel, his only child, or to Edsel's children.[46]

The Wealth Tax of 1935 captured Ford's attention, if not his wealth.

He was 72 years old and refused to turn over two-thirds of his estate to the government. His lawyers advised him that one way out of his tax problems was to set up the Ford Foundation. Gifts to foundations were tax deductible, so Ford could dump his fortune in the Ford Foundation, put Edsel in charge of it, and thereby save $321 million in inheritance taxes and keep his business in the family.[47]

Ford's maneuver preserved family control of his company, but it took his capital out of investment, froze it in the foundation, and put it, after his death, in the hands of the bureaucratic types he had fought all his life. For example, Ford hated college-educated "experts," but two of the four associate directors of the Ford Foundation were Robert Hutchins, chancellor of the University of Chicago, and Milton Katz, law professor at Harvard University. The other two were former New Dealers: Chester Davis, former head of the Agricultural Adjustment Administration, and H. Rowan Gaither, who had worked in the Farm Credit Administration. Raymond Moley, a New Dealer who turned conservative, scoffed at the "projectitis" of the foundations, and its "big and expensive staff of busy people who think up and sort out innumerable projects, to be bestowed with plenty of money upon specially created agencies or upon professors hard pressed to live on their academic salaries." As historian Allan Nevins observed, "In a real sense, Henry Ford's factory, his fortune, his life-work, had been socialized."[48]

The New Deal programs and the freezing of Ford's wealth naturally irritated him; what infuriated him, however, was the thought of labor unions in his factories. The presence of unions meant the loss of control, and the loss of control, to Ford, meant the end of his entrepreneurship.

Ford looked at the issue this way. His use of mass production helped him satisfy human needs in unprecedented ways. He could make high quality cars, sell them at low prices, and at the same time pay very high wages. But to do this he had to control his own destiny. He had to weigh market conditions and cut prices, raise wages, or reduce working hours when he thought the timing was right.[49]

The presence of unions, Ford argued, disrupted the whole process. For one thing, it gave labor the first fruits of mass production—ahead of the consumer and even the entrepreneur. If unions hiked wages, called strikes, and regulated output, the consumers lost their cheap cars and Ford lost a first-rate business. Ford insisted that he needed the freedom to take risks, just as laborers needed the freedom to stay at his company or leave if they had better offers. Under this system, Ford tried to sell—pound for pound—the cheapest and most utilitarian industrial product in America and pay his workers the highest wages of their kind anywhere in the world.[50]

During the 1910s and 1920s, Ford's system worked marvelously. The Model T ruled the highways. And workers by the tens of thousands flocked to Ford's factories at Highland Park and River Rouge. The five (and later six) dollar day and the forty-hour week became standard at his plants. Turnover was low, morale was high, and unions almost invisible.

The Great Depression, however, destroyed Ford's system. It ruined the market for cars; then, when massive layoffs and wage cuts became inevitable, Roosevelt and the courts approved the Wagner Act, which gave labor the right of collective bargaining. Ford, who turned 70 in 1933, was unable to cope with these changes. Perhaps he was in mental decline. Allan Nevins called it "a distinct hardening of the moral arteries." In his younger days, Ford would walk along the assembly line, talk with workers, and help them sometimes with their jobs. By the 1930s, he was avoiding them. "A great business is really too big to be human," Ford decided. "If we are overcrowded, get rid of some people."[51]

Low morale began to set in at Ford Motor Company. Massive layoffs made men fearful for their jobs. Cuts in wages also discouraged the workers. Then came the speed up of the assembly line—and also the stretch out (where men had to tend more machines). The rules were meticulously enforced: no sitting, no talking, no whistling, and no smoking. Lunch breaks were only 15 minutes long, as workers rushed to stuff their mouths with food, use the toilet, and wash up. Job turnover increased; many men couldn't stand it.[52]

Meanwhile, Ford seemed to lose his ability to judge character. His son Edsel—not a great leader but a competent one—was supposed to inherit the company, but Henry humiliated him and regularly overruled him on key issues. For example, the older Ford put Harry Bennett, an ex-boxer and navy man, in charge of labor relations. Ford had originally hired Bennett to protect his family from outside threats and potential kidnappers. From there, Bennett wormed his way into management and won Ford's complete confidence.[53]

Bennett was a ruffian, not a diplomat. He had strong underworld connections and loved to intimidate. He always kept a pistol handy and practiced target shooting in his office—where he also kept two lion cubs. More than 800 men worked for Bennett in the "Ford Service Department," and they combed the factories eager to enforce the rules, fire the negligent, and pummel the unionizers. Critics of Bennett's gestapo sometimes passed nasty notes down the assembly line; Bennett, therefore, salted the line with spies who tattled on coworkers and stifled union sentiments. When the United Auto Workers (UAW) showed up near the overpass at the River Rouge, Bennett's service department was there to punch and kick them, smash their cameras, and chase them away. If the Great Depression opened the door to labor strife, Henry Ford invited it in when he empowered Harry Bennett.[54]

Bennett's bullying tactics only delayed the inevitable and made it worse: Ford Motor Company would be unionized. The Wagner Act had swung the law in favor of organized labor; and public sympathy against Ford's spies and the speed up made the law easier to enforce. Ford had a severe stroke in 1938 and increasingly lost touch with reality. No longer were his wages the highest of their kind in America. In fact, by the late 1930s, they had dropped below those paid at General Motors and Chrysler.[55]

In April 1941, a massive walkout at River Rouge forced Ford to agree to a union election before he could reopen the plant. In May, the election was held and the UAW captured 70 percent of the vote. The older American Federation of Labor received 27 percent; and Ford's antiunion position won only 2.6 percent of the votes. Ford, whose mind was more in the 1920s than the 1940s, was surprised and crushed at the result. As Charles Sorensen, Ford's production manager, said, it was "perhaps the greatest disappointment he had in all his business experience; . . . he was never the same after that." Ford threatened to close the company, but was advised that if he did the government would reopen it to fulfill his defense contracts. The free-enterprise era was over; he had to negotiate with the UAW.[56]

In the bargaining that followed, the UAW leaders won more personal liberty for the typical Ford worker. A man's labor, they argued, is his property and that property ought to have some protection. Spies in the factory, therefore, would now have to identify themselves, which meant the Ford Service Department had to wear special uniforms. Also, the speed up was a threat to health and dignity and would have to go.[57]

The UAW, however, went beyond these points of personal liberty and won further concessions that stifled freedom of choice and the functioning of a free society. Not only did all Ford workers have to join a union, they had to join the UAW whether they wanted to or not. What's more, all initiation fees, monthly dues, and special charges had to be deducted for the UAW by Ford. Finally, what wages to pay would no longer be a decision of management, or of market forces. Ford promised to adjust wages "to the highest level of any competitor select-ed by the UAW," regardless of the productivity of the workers. This UAW contract was the most stringent it had ever secured, and it paved the way for more benefits later. As Garet Garrett observed, "Where before workers were not permitted to smoke anywhere on the premis-es or to lounge at ease when the assembly line broke down, now they dragged in vats of victory beer, played craps in their leisure moments, [and] smoked as they liked. . . ." [58]

Shortly after signing the UAW contract, Ford had another stroke. He was unfit to run the company, but he refused to loosen his grip on it. Edsel died in 1943, which meant that his oldest son Henry Ford II was groomed for the presidency. Among the first acts of young Ford, after firing Harry Bennett, were pacifying the UAW and working with the government to remove the price-fixing powers of the Office of Price Administration after World War II. His world of government reg-ulation, government mandates, and the UAW was different from that of his grandfather's. The original Henry Ford had lived in two eras: His astonishing victories in the first era were diminished in the second.[59]

7

Empires of Service

THE WORD "EMPIRE" COMES FROM THE LATIN WORDS "IMPERIUM," OR dominion, and from "imperare," which means to command. The best entrepreneurs fulfill these terms. They dominate their industries and extend their command into new territories around the world. From a central location, or capital, they expand their markets and control their industries—not by force but by service: selling products that customers want at competitive prices.

From 1850 to 1930, the U. S. went from being a second-rate economic power to leading the world in most crucial industries. A key part of the American triumph occurred in Michigan. In 1850, the young state of Michigan was cold, remote, and swampy. Its finances, after a failed railroad-building scheme, were shaky and its future bleak. But by the early 1900s, Michigan's empire builders—especially Henry Crapo, William Durant, Herbert Dow, Will Kellogg, and Henry Ford—had transformed the state's economy. Michigan was the world center for auto production and a major exporter of products as diverse as chemicals, furniture, and breakfast cereals.

What can we say about Michigan's empire builders as a group? At one level, they employed Michigan's natural resources to the fullest. Herbert Dow tapped the brine in the Saginaw Valley and used it to make products from bleach to explosives to magnesium engines. Henry Crapo and others helped Michigan become the top lumber-producing state in the Union. William Durant, Crapo's grandson, helped lead the diversification from lumber to carriages. His Durant-Dort Carriage Company, which used a lot of Michigan lumber, became the largest carriage company in the nation. Durant later diversified into cars, founded General Motors, and gave America the Buick and Chevrolet. Henry Ford, his counterpart, popularized the auto and "put America on wheels" with his Model T. Ford, Durant, and Dow all built worldwide empires to market and sell their products.

Other Michigan entrepreneurs created products from resources available that had nothing to do with Michigan. Will Kellogg and his brother, John Harvey Kellogg, invented food items such as peanut butter and cornflakes. Will, with his marketing genius, made flaked cereals a breakfast habit throughout the nation. To a lesser extent, Dr. William Upjohn and Dan Gerber forged empires by making vitamin pills and baby food.

Several points are striking about Michigan's remarkable group of entrepreneurs. First, they built their empires locally—in places like Flint, Midland, Battle Creek, and Dearborn—but expanded them into the nation and then the world. Many middle-class families, whether in New York, Paris, or Buenos Aires, ate cornflakes for breakfast, drove Chevys to work, and used Dow's bleach on their clothes and his bromine for sedatives. Kellogg, Durant, Dow, and Ford, like Astor in an earlier generation, built empires that shaped the world long after their deaths.

Second, this group was remarkably inventive and creative. They not only took risks and carved out markets, but they invented many of the key products needed to establish their empires of service. Dow heads the list with his 107 patents, but Ford and Kellogg were, in some ways, even more impressive. Kellogg, with help from his brother, practically invented the whole flaked-cereal industry. His example inspired others, and from Rice Krispies to All-Bran, Kellogg cereals set the standard. Henry Ford, among other things, invented the V-8 engine and assembled the team that made plate glass from a continuous ribbon with no hand work. More than this, his whole company was for years an experiment in creativity—from the assembly line to raising wages to cutting work hours. Not surprisingly, the man who was probably Ford's best friend was Thomas Edison. Only with Edison, who began his science experiments during his youth in Port Huron, Michigan, did Ford meet his match in creativity.

The inventiveness of Michigan's entrepreneurs is part of what separates them from so many of their peers elsewhere. John D. Rockefeller, for example, was a genius at organizing oil production, but he was not an inventor. Andrew Carnegie led the American steel industry to world dominance, but he also was no inventor. Rather, he applied what others invented, such as the open-hearth method of steelmaking and new accounting techniques.

In the case of Henry Ford, the whole auto industry marveled at his unique creative impulses. The brilliance of his mind on issues of technology (not politics) was a regular topic of conversation among his imitators. "How did he do it?" was the usual question. The "it," as Garet Garrett observed, was "the existence of an nth faculty, a mysterious gadget that worked without ticking, and produced the unexpected answer." William Knudsen, Ford's production manager, was once in a "How did he do it?" conversation, and Knudsen answered this way:

> Say we are going to buy a certain part for the automobile instead of making it for ourselves, maybe the distributor head, an assembled part made up of many pieces. The samples come in. The production men, the engineers and the

technicians spend days going over them, taking them apart, testing one against another, making notes and tying labels to them. Then they are all spread out on a table, maybe thirty of them, ready for Ford. He comes in, looks at them for two or three minutes with his squinted eyes, says, 'That one,' and walks out. It's that one, sure enough. But how does he do it?[1]

However Ford did "it," his inventiveness, his creativity, and his knack for making cars was what separated him from the others in the auto industry.

A third point about Michigan's entrepreneurs is that they wanted to build empires more than they wanted to make money. Of course, the two usually go together. But making a distinction between them is critical to understanding the mind of Michigan's early entrepreneurs. Money, or capital, was valued by these entrepreneurs not as an end but as a means to create an economic empire. In the same way, weapons are valued by an army not as an end but as a means to conquer people and territory. Weapons are tools for the soldier in the same way that capital is a tool for the entrepreneur. The big difference here is that an army creates and expands its empire by force; entrepreneurs create and expand their empires by service to others. A soldier controls by using weapons to threaten violence; an entrepreneur persuades by using capital to offer good products at low prices.

The big challenge to entrepreneurs in an undeveloped state like Michigan was raising capital. John Jacob Astor made his money in New York and plowed it into Michigan. Henry Crapo forged a complex network for wheedling capital from his cautious friends in New Bedford and Boston, Massachusetts. Herbert Dow lobbied established businessmen in Cleveland for his capital. Will Kellogg needed help from a large investor in St. Louis. By the early 1900s, some Michigan cities were rich enough to support their own entrepreneurs. Henry Ford, with mixed success, solicited a variety of investors in Detroit. William Durant tapped the bankers of Flint—first to build carriages, and later Chevrolets.

With capital in hand, the next step was mobilizing workers behind tough and compelling goals. For Ford, the task was building a reliable car so cheaply that all middle-class Americans could afford it. For Dow, the issue was survival—how to make bleach, bromine, and dyes cheap enough to match the strong European cartels. Kellogg and Durant started with high quality products, so the challenge was in marketing: how to get every American to eat a bowl of cornflakes, or ride in a blue ribbon carriage.

Workers, like soldiers, will usually follow if the leader knows how to lead. The prevailing theory of management said that employees must be controlled, directed, and closely supervised. Michigan's entrepreneurs, by contrast, tended to give their workers freedom to create, personal responsibility for hard tasks, and rewards and bonuses for jobs well done. Henry Ford wanted the best workers in Michigan, and he launched the five-dollar day to get them. Will Kellogg liked to reward worthy employees with a handshake that contained a $20 bill. Herbert Dow might argue loudly with his chemists, but he trusted their abilities, paid them well, and turned them loose to invent and create.

Fourth, Michigan's empire builders all followed Biblical principles, even though not all of them were Christians. As George Gilder has observed,

> "Do unto others as you would have them do unto you" and
> "Give and you will be given unto" are the central rules of the
> life of enterprise. They require the institutions of property
> (you cannot give what you do not own) and personal free-
> dom (a planned economy cannot allow the surprising gifts
> of entrepreneurs). But it is a life that most deeply springs
> from religious faith and culture. The act of thrift, suppress-

ing your own desires in order to serve the desires of others—the act of committing your work and wealth, over a period of years, to bring into the world a new good that the world may well reject—the act of putting your own fate into the hands of unknown others, freely deciding your future in a market of free choice—these are the essential acts of a religious person.[2]

The faith of these empire builders was always tested. They all either went bankrupt, or verged on it at some critical point in their lives. In no case did they experience the steady growth and predictable success that one might have expected from talented men with good and popular products to sell. They took leaps of faith, fell flat on their faces, then desperately changed their tactics and tried to raise new capital to stay afloat.

Herbert Dow, for example, failed in his first business venture; in his second, he was ousted from control. On his third try, he went into the bleach business, and he calculated his costs of production very carefully. Then came the unexpected. He was immediately challenged by a British cartel, which cut its price for bleach in half. Dow had to find ways to slash costs even more or he would fail a third time. When Will Kellogg finally broke loose from the San, he calculated his costs of making cornflakes. What he didn't count on was having his factory burn down and his main competitor buy up all the new equipment for making cereal. Henry Crapo floundered in the lumber business until he doubled his risks, bought some sawmills, and began to process and market his own wood. Only after years of cutting costs, improving their products, and removing bottlenecks did these men make sudden breakthroughs. In no cases did their businesses show immediate and steady growth.

Hindsight makes their accomplishments seem easy and inevitable. After all, one can reason, the technology of the 1890s made motor cars possible. The speed and efficiency of cars versus that of horses and carriages made the triumph of the auto inevitable. Therefore, Henry Ford was just someone in the right place at the right time.

What this casual analysis overlooks is the reality that faced Henry Ford and every other maker of vehicles at the turn of the century.

In the first place, over fifty auto firms in the U. S. alone made cars in 1900. Most of these vehicles ran by steam, which was potentially economical, or by electricity, which Thomas Edison predicted would power the cars of the future. Henry Ford rejected both of these options. Instead, he invested in an internal combustion gasoline-powered car—and he did so before the development of no-knock gasoline.

Second, the carriage business was still expanding as late as 1906. Most experts saw the car as dangerous, unreliable, or impossibly expensive for most Americans. "The horse is here to stay, but the automobile is only a novelty—a fad," said the president of the Michigan Savings Bank to Henry Ford's lawyer in 1903.[3]

Third, within the market for cars with internal combustion engines, Buicks outsold Model Ts before 1910. Ford's key move in 1910 was cutting the price of his cars by almost 20 percent—and watching his sales almost double. For many years thereafter, he cut the price, improved the quality of his car, and watched sales skyrocket. This strategy was an act of faith. "We have never considered any costs as fixed," Ford said. "Therefore we first reduce the price to a point where *we believe* (my emphasis) more sales will result. Then we go ahead and *try* (my emphasis again) to make the price. We do not bother about the costs [of production]. The new price forces the costs down."[4] These five sentences describe one of the most revolutionary acts in American history. Ford just explained how he was able to supply cars for the tens of millions of Americans who wanted them.

The fifth trait of Michigan's empire builders was their fierce independence and their aversion to monopoly and to government solutions to problems. Even before statehood, John Jacob Astor displayed this independence with his American Fur Company when he challenged the government fur factories. In the 1840s, the subsidized railroad disaster brought the issue of government intervention to the top of the state's agenda. The next two generations of Michigan entrepreneurs were among the most independent that our nation has ever produced. When Henry Crapo was governor, his defense of the Constitution of 1850 was intense. He sacrificed popularity, party loyalty, and even his health so that he could veto bill after bill that allowed Michigan cities to subsidize local railroads. Crapo was an expert in attracting outside capital into Michigan and he knew the dangers that subsidizing railroads posed to individual liberty and to the integrity and credit rating of his adopted state.

In 1919, fifty years after Crapo's death, his grandson William Durant was president of General Motors. In a speech that year, Durant sounded just like his grandfather:

> Competition is the life of trade. I stand for competition. I am opposed to monopoly or control on the principle that it destroys initiative, curtails freedom of action, and frequently leads to abuse of power. In a controlled situation, the people take what they can get. In a competitive situation, the people get what they want.

> If I controlled the motor car business, the public would very likely get what I cared to build. With open competition, as we now have it, the people will get what they want. If I do not supply it, my competitors will.[5]

Durant's chief competitor, Henry Ford, could not have agreed more. Ford, in fact, was one of the main reasons the auto industry was so free of monopoly and government control. He alone challenged George Selden's patent on gasoline engines. Without Ford, the

Association of Licensed Automobile Manufacturers (A.L.A.M.), which held Selden's patent, could and did deny licenses to carmakers. The A. L. A. M. restricted entry into the auto business and imposed charges on all members. Ford's long and well-reasoned challenge to the A. L. A. M. in the courts liberated the auto industry from the monopolists.

With the auto industry free of restrictions on entry and government regulations, the price of cars steadily dropped during the 1910s and 1920s. The pressure of competition improved the quality of cars dramatically—automatic starters, hydraulic brakes, and gas gauges became standard by 1930. With Ford and General Motors locked in combat, the American consumer was the winner. Vehicle sales soared from 181,000 in 1910 to over 5,000,000 in 1929. Trucks for moving freight were part of this rise. The railroad industry, with its price fixing and government controls, lost passenger and freight traffic to the auto industry steadily after about 1920. Henry Ford, in fact, bought and operated the Detroit, Toledo, and Ironton Railroad during the 1920s, but sold it in 1929 largely because he loathed the regulations and government interference into how he ran his business. In the auto industry, win or lose, he had complete freedom to design, build and price his cars and compete openly with fellow Michiganians in what had become America's largest growth industry.

In the 1930s, Ford became the center of opposition to President Roosevelt's NRA. Roosevelt and his New Dealers urged the auto companies to join together to regulate wages, prices, and hours of work. Ford alone refused to join. With Durant out at General Motors, Ford didn't have his fellow individualist to join him. When the federal bureaucrats refused to accept Ford's low bids on government contracts, Ford ignored them and survived on private-sector business. The irony here is that Ford already led American industry in paying high wages. Why should a government agency set minimum wages, Ford wondered, when he set the standard long before the 1930s? Referring to the NRA auto code, Ford said, "If we tried to live up to it we would have to live down to it."[6] Before the government could coerce Ford into joining the NRA's auto cartel, however, the Supreme Court stepped in and declared the NRA unconstitutional.

If possible, Herbert Dow opposed government activism even more strongly than Ford did (except for protective tariffs). In fact, Dow first built his chemical empire by challenging government-supported monopolies. In the 1890s, when Dow entered the chemical business, the British and especially the Germans had long dominated the chemical industry—and their governments encouraged them to form cartels and control prices and production. American chemical companies not only lagged far behind Europe, they often faced predatory price cutting whenever they sold abroad. Some American companies, like DuPont, carved niches in special markets such as gunpowder. But Dow was the first American to openly challenge the Europeans where they were already established—in areas like bleach, bromides, and indigo.

In doing so, Dow gave the world a model demonstration in how to defeat predatory price cutting. Before Dow, many people could argue against oligopolies this way: "If a corporation is big enough, it can cut prices below cost, drive out its small competitors, and then raise prices to whatever it wants to charge. Therefore, we need government regulation, antitrust laws perhaps, to control large greedy corporations." Dow showed how a small company could beat the large monopolist. In the bromine industry, the Germans cut prices below cost with the specific intent of destroying Dow. In response, Dow secretly bought the cheap German bromides, repackaged them, and sold them at a profit in markets around the world. During the early 1900s, Dow regularly expanded his chemical empire when the Germans tried to reap large profits from their cartels in indigo, magnesium, and other products.

The 1920s was the last decade when an empire could be built without major interference from the federal government. With the Great

Depression came the rapid expanding of federal powers. The Smoot-Hawley Tariff, passed in 1930, was the most restrictive tariff in U. S. history. The Reconstruction Finance Corporation had the government financing banks, railroads, and other industries. The Agricultural Adjustment Act regulated farm production; the National Industrial Recovery Act regulated most corporations—except for the Ford Motor Company. And later the Wagner Act shifted the balance of power from the entrepreneurs to the labor unions.

The tax revenues needed to pay for these and other new programs were astonishing. The top federal tax rate in 1930 was 24 percent. In 1932, under President Hoover, the rate was hiked to 63 percent. Under President Roosevelt the rate was first raised to 79 percent and later jumped to over 90 percent. Large inheritance taxes also emerged to scoop up what the income tax missed. During the 1930s, the empire builders were, in effect, asked to send their empires to Washington.

Herbert Dow died in 1930, before he could denounce such a request. William Durant lost his fortune on the stock market, before Washing-ton could confiscate it. Ford and Kellogg chose to shelter their wealth from the swirling storms from Washington. With the Ford and Kellogg Foundations quickly in place, they had preserved their empires, but they were no longer the commanders. The era of laissez faire was over. As Garet Garrett concluded, "You may like it better this way. Many people do. In any case, it was not to be argued. Only this—that if laissez faire had not begotten the richest world that ever existed there would have been much less for the welfare state to distribute."[7]

One of Michigan's greatest entrepreneurs, William Durant, helped shift the state's export base from lumber to carriages and from carriages to cars. Even before autos came along, Flint was known as "The Vehicle City."

Appendix

Michigan Entrepreneurs vs. The Textbooks

OST TEXTBOOKS IN U.S. HISTORY, AND EVEN THOSE IN MICHIGAN history, seem to ignore the lessons that Michigan's experience teaches. Most college U.S. history texts, for example, reverse the Michigan lesson: They argue that entrepreneurs, not the state, created problems for society. According to *These United States* by Irwin Unger, a Pulitzer-prize winner, the image of entrepreneurs "is, in many ways, a negative one: The business leaders of this period were 'robber barons' who held the nation for ransom to amass their great fortunes; they were crude and vulgar men who flaunted their wealth and their bad taste." Government intervention, in this view, was needed to protect the public from the allegedly greedy businessmen.[1]

The major point of confusion in this robber baron view of history is that it fails to separate *market entrepreneurs,* who tried to succeed by creating and marketing a superior product at a low cost, and *political entrepreneurs,* who tried to succeed by using government to give them an advantage.[2] Market entrepreneurs were men like Henry Ford and Herbert Dow, whose cars and chemicals helped make America the top industrial power in the world. They gave the world new and exciting products at competitive prices. Political entrepreneurs include Thomas McKenney, who headed the government fur company, and Levi Humphrey, a builder for the Michigan Southern Railroad. They stifled productivity (through monopolies and price fixing), corrupted business and politics, and hindered economic development in Michigan.

Even textbooks in Michigan history seem confused about the effects of government intervention in Michigan's economic life. An example is Willis F. Dunbar and George S. May's *Michigan: A History of the Wolverine State*, which is the leading college text on Michigan history. The authors do describe the financial problems of the state-subsidized railroads. Then comes this paragraph:

> On the positive side, however, there can be no doubt that railroad development in Michigan progressed more rapidly as a result of the state's actions than it would have done without. Private efforts at railroad construction which had been under way for over a half a decade before the state launched its program, had scarcely any tangible results, but the *demonstrated success of the state-operated central, and to a lesser extent, the southern railroads* (my emphasis), created the interest among substantial investors that was needed to develop privately-operated lines in Michigan.[3]

If the state-operated railroads were so successful, why were they losing money? Why did they have to be immediately rebuilt by the private owners? Why did the legislature vote to sell them for about $860,000 less than it spent to build them? These questions suggest that the state-funded railroads were not successful.

In *Michigan: A History of the Great Lakes State*, Bruce Rubenstein and Lawrence E. Ziewacz rightly call the state-operated railroads a "tragedy." However, they blame the hard times of the late 1830s, not the state funding. In fact, they say, "It was so obvious that state funding was the only solution" to building the railroads.[4] Certainly, the Panic of 1837 made credit harder to get; and President Jackson's "Specie Circular" tied up cash by requiring payment in silver or gold for federal lands. But the lesson that Michigan learned was that state-operated railroads were inherently inefficient regardless of the nation's prosperity. That is what Governor Mason came to recognize when he called the idea of using the state to build railroads "that false spirit of the age." When politicians choose which cities to include on the route, who to hire, and which company to buy materials from, the process is always politicized and wasteful of tax dollars. Unlike entrepreneurs, Michigan's legislators were responsible to their districts, not to profits and losses.

Some historians argue that the railroad problem in Michigan was one of too little government. In *Democracy's Railroads: Public Enterprise in Jacksonian Michigan,* Robert Parks has written the only book on Michigan's state-built railroads. In his conclusion, he argues that his book "points to the need for national planning, and the reduction of local influences in decision making."[5] The idea here is that politicians in Washington would have been more enlightened than those in Lansing. In the 1860s, however, these Washington politicians had their chance at railroad building when they organized the building and funding of three transcontinental railroads. All three, however, had the same problems as Michigan's state-funded railroads: They were poorly built; they were unprofitable; and they all went bankrupt shortly after they were completed. The one transcontinental that was well built and did not go bankrupt was the only one that received no federal funding—James J. Hill's Great Northern Railroad.[6]

Perhaps it is hard for modern historians, who take activist governments for granted, to appreciate the agony that Michigan's early leaders went through in their search for the proper role of government in economic development. These leaders knew that their decision would

The development of the lumber industry was Michigan's first test of the state's commitment to laissez-faire.

forever shape the future of their state. Starting with Governor Mason in his "false spirit of the age" speech, we can see the Michigan governors—whether Whig or Democrat—moving toward consensus. William Woodbridge, the governor who followed Mason, first suggested selling the railroads to entrepreneurs. Governor John Barry, who was elected after Woodbridge, concluded that "in extraordinary cases only . . . should a state undertake the construction of public works." Governor Alpheus Felch, who followed Barry, helped complete the sale of the railroads to private owners. "The business of transporting passengers and freight by railroads," Felch bluntly stated, "is clearly not within the ordinary design of state government." Experience had been a rigorous teacher and the battle of ideas was won by the market entrepreneurs.

The development of the lumber industry would be the first test of Michigan's commitment to laissez-faire. As Michigan became the leading lumber state, some critics emerged and argued for public ownership, or at least restricted cutting of the state's timber. They made the following charges. First, the lumber barons were harvesting so much lumber that Michigan's forests were rapidly disappearing. Second, the cutting was so inefficient that much of the wood was being wasted. Third, some landowners were cutting the timber off their land and then abandoning it without paying taxes on it.

The state resisted the temptation to regulate, however, and here were the results. First, the rapid cutting of Michigan's pine forests did eventually raise prices for lumber, which encouraged conservation and the replanting of trees. New forests have steadily re-emerged and Michigan is again a major lumber state.[7] Second, waste in harvesting lumber was part of learning the business. Innovations in saws, railroads, and marketing in the late 1800s reduced the waste and made the business more profitable. Third, the benefits of attracting entrepreneurs, who exported and processed the state's lumber, offset the occasional loss in property tax revenues when timber was quickly cut.

This last point is critical. We have seen how Henry Crapo brought in capital from Massachusetts and used it to build the city of Flint. And without Crapo, Michigan would not have had his grandson, who helped shift the state's export base from lumber to carriages and from carriages to cars. Other cities also used their lumber effectively. Entrepreneurs in Grand Rapids made their city a center for fine furniture. Also, George Pullman, who became a large exporter of railroad cars, had his start in Grand Rapids before moving his business to Detroit. The city of Pontiac became a center for wagon making; other entrepreneurs built large shipyards in Bay City, Port Huron, and Grand Haven. Muskegon and Saginaw were built around their lumber industries and entrepreneurs there diversified into foundries, railroads, passenger cars, and other products. By 1900, the lumber boom in Michigan was over, but many cities were poised for future growth because of their start with lumber.[8]

As the lumber industry moved west, some states experimented with public ownership. An example from Washington shows the pitfalls that Michigan avoided. In 1887, Mr. and Mrs. W. W. Beck bought many acres of timberland in the suburbs of Seattle. They so much enjoyed the giant fir trees on their land that they converted it into a park with foot paths, benches, totem poles, and even a pavilion for concerts. Ravenna Park became so popular that, even with admission charges, 8,000 to 10,000 people would visit it on busy days. In 1911, sentiment for public ownership increased and Seattle annexed Ravenna Park and paid the Becks $135,633 for their land. Under city ownership, however, the large fir trees began to disappear. By 1925, they were all gone, and after an investigation, the city charged the superintendent with abuse of public funds and the unauthorized sale of park property. Under public ownership of Ravenna Park, as with the public ownership of Michigan's early railroads, the bureaucrats had no incentive to care for the property, protect it, and increase its value. Under the Becks in Seattle and the Crapos in Flint, the owners had incentives to care for the land, use it wisely, and replant if necessary.

Endnotes

Introduction

1. M. I. Finley, *The Portable Greek Historians: The Essence of Herodotus, Thucydides, Xenophon, Polybius* (New York: The Viking Press, 1960), 266-67.

2. Leonard Engel, *Medicine Makers of Kalamazoo* (New York: McGraw-Hill, 1961).

3. Joseph J. Fucini and Suzy Fucini, *Entrepreneurs: The Men and Women behind Famous Brand Names and How They Made It* (Boston: G. K. Hall, 1985), 66-69.

4. David B. McConnell, *Forging the Peninsulas* (Hillsdale, Mich.: Hillsdale Educational Publishers, 1995), 179-80.

5. Ernie and Jill Couch, *Michigan Trivia* (Nashville: Rutledge Hill Press, 1989), 77, 78, 94; and Willis F. Dunbar and George S. May, *Michigan: A History of the Wolverine State* (Grand Rapids, Mich.: Eerdmans Publishing Co., 1980), 476, 478-79.

6. Burton Folsom, "Remembering the 'Real McCoy'," *The Detroit News*, February 28, 1996.

7. Reginald Larrie, "Minorities Make Their Mark," in Mike Davis, *The Technology Century* (Detroit: Engineering Technology Publishing, 1995), 103.

8. Luke 6:38 and Mark 9:35.

Chapter One

1. Horatio Alger, Jr. (1832-1899) wrote almost 120 novels that sold about 17 million copies, and maybe more. For a good introduction to Alger, see *Ragged Dick and Mark, The Match Boy: Two Novels* (New York: Collier Books, 1962).

2. Two classic works on the fur trade are Hiram M. Chittenden, *The American Fur Trade of the Far West*, 2 vols. (Lincoln: University of Nebraska Press, [1901] 1986); and Paul C. Phillips, *The Fur Trade*, 2 vols. (Norman: University of Oklahoma Press, 1961).

3. Good accounts of the early fur trade are found in Chittenden, *American Fur Trade* and Phillips, *Fur Trade*.

4. Francis Paul Prucha, *The Great Father: The United States Government and the American Indians* (Lincoln: University of Nebraska Press, 1986), 31-36.

5. Ibid., 35-40. Phillips, *Fur Trade*, II, 76.

6. Prucha, *Great Father,* 35-40; Chittenden, *American Fur Trade*, I, 12-15.

7. Herman J. Viola, *Thomas L. McKenney: Architect of America's Early Indian Policy, 1816-1830* (Chicago: Swallow Press, 1974), 5.

8. Ibid., 2, 25-26; Phillips, *Fur Trade,* II, 76.

9. Viola, *McKenney,* 13, 25-26, 48-49, 68-69.

10. An early and usually reliable biography of Astor is Kenneth Wiggins Porter, *John Jacob Astor: Businessman,* 2 vols. (Cambridge: Harvard University Press, 1931). A useful short essay is William James Ghent, "John Jacob Astor," in Allen Johnson, ed., *Dictionary of American Biography* (New York: Charles Scribner's Sons, 1957), I, 397-99. The most reliable and most informative book on Astor is John Denis Haeger, *John Jacob Astor: Business and Finance in the Early Republic* (Detroit: Wayne State University Press, 1991).

11. Haeger, *Astor,* 42-43, 46-56, 63.

12. Ibid., 57-60, 78-92, 203-04, 230-32.

13. Ibid., 57, 59, 67, 78.

14. Carolyn Gilman, *Where Two Worlds Meet: The Great Lakes Fur Trade* (St. Paul: Minnesota Historical Society, 1982).

15. Haeger, *Astor,* 99-102, 105, 185-88, 205-43.

16. Porter, *Astor,* 711-12. An excellent and reliable historical novel that shows the fur trade in action is Kenneth Roberts, *Northwest Passage* (New York: Doubleday, 1937).

17. Gilman, *Where Two Worlds Meet,* 86; Haeger, *Astor,* 9, 13-14, 186.

18. Haeger, *Astor,* 14, 25-26, 68.

19. Viola, *McKenney,* 34.

20. Haeger, *Astor,* 238-39.

21. Ibid., 213, 221, 223.

22. Ibid., 228-29, 232-33; Porter, *Astor,* 589-638.

23. Viola, *McKenney,* 16-17, 19-20, 35, 48.

24. Porter, *Astor,* 686-790; Haeger, *Astor,* 226-27, 237.

25. Phillips, *Fur Trade,* II, 87; Viola, *McKenney,* 48, 54-55.

26. Viola, *McKenney,* 55.

27. Ibid., 57.

28. Ibid., 59; Prucha, *The Great Father,* 39; Phillips, *Fur Trade,* II, 89.

29. Viola, *McKenney*, 34-35, 56-57.

30. Ibid., 55-56; Porter, *Astor*, 706-07, 712-13; Haeger, *Astor*, 193; Phillips, *Fur Trade*, II, 69.

31. Haeger, *Astor*, 233-34.

32. Ibid., 208, 210-11; Prucha, *The Great Father*, 38.

33. Viola, *McKenney*, 57-58.

34. Ibid., 61.

35. Ibid.

36. Ibid., 48, 64; Haeger, *Astor*, 196-98, 209; Ida A. Johnson, *The Michigan Fur Trade* (Lansing: Michigan Historical Commission, 1919), 147-48.

37. Viola, *McKenney*, 48, 61-62.

38. Jedidiah Morse, *A Report to the Secretary of War* (Washington, D. C.: Davis and Force, 1822), 12.

39. Ibid., 13-15.

40. Ibid., 56.

41. Ibid., 61.

42. Viola, *McKenney*, 68-69; Thomas Hart Benton, *Thirty Years View* (New York: D. Appleton & Co., 1854), I, 13, 20-21.

43. Phillips, *Fur Trade*, II, 94-95.Viola, McKenney, 68-69; Benton, *Thirty Years View*, I, 20-21.

44. Viola, *McKenney*, 71-80 (quotations on pp. 74, 76). Francis Paul Prucha, *Lewis Cass and American Indian Policy* (Detroit: Wayne State University Press, 1967), 10-11.

45. Viola, *McKenney*, 80.

46. Haeger, *Astor*, 220-23, 232-38.

47. Ibid., 234; Prucha, *Lewis Cass*, 10-11.

48. Haeger, *Astor*, 236.

49. Ibid., 107-09, 186, 236.

50. Ibid., 238-40.

51. Ibid., 236-37; Viola, *McKenney*, 201.

52. Viola, *McKenney*, 92-95.

53. Ibid., 98, 176.

54. Ibid., 173-75.

55. Ibid., 200-03.

56. Haeger, *Astor,* 242-43, 244-79, 282.

57. Viola, *McKenney,* 223, 268-77, 281, 292, 295-300.

Chapter Two

1. Willis F. Dunbar and George S. May, *Michigan: A History of the Wolverine State* (Grand Rapids, Mich.: Eerdmans Publishing Co., 1980), 222; Lawton T. Hemans, *Life and Times of Stevens Thomson Mason* (Lansing: Michigan Historical Commission, 1920), 17,55..

2. Two books have been written on Mason. They are Hemans, *Mason;* and Kent Sagendorph, *Stevens Thomson Mason: Misunderstood Patriot* (New York: E. P. Dutton & Co., 1947).

3. For the material in this and the next five paragraphs on Mason's early life, see Hemans, *Mason,* 11-37; and Sagendorph, *Mason,* 15-73.

4. Hemans, *Mason,* 23-34; Sagendorph, *Mason,* 59-67, 76.

5. Sagendorph, *Mason,* 86-89; Andrew C. McLaughlin, *Lewis Cass* (Boston: Houghton Mifflin, 1899); Frank B. Woodford, *Lewis Cass: The Last Jeffersonian* (New York: Octagon Books, 1973).

6. JoEllen Vinyard, *The Irish on the Urban Frontier: Detroit, 1850-1880* (New York: Arno Press, 1976), 18.

7. Sagendorph, *Mason,* 121-22, 126-31; Woodford, *Lewis Cass,* 187-89.

8. Sagendorph, *Mason,* 135-40.

9. Ibid., 141-43. Emily V. Mason, Governor Mason's sister, has written a valuable account of the Mason administration. See Emily V. Mason, "Chapters from the Autobiography of an Octogenarian, 1830-1850," *Michigan Pioneer and Historical Society* 35 (1905), 248-58.

10. Sagendorph, *Mason,* 142.

11. Ibid., 143-44.

12. Ibid., 147-48.

13. Ibid., 175.

14. Ibid., 22, 45-46; Helen Hill, "George Mason," *Dictionary of American Biography* (New York: Charles Scribner's Sons), VI, 361-64.

15. Mason, "Autobiography," 248; Sagendorph, *Mason,* 155-62.

16. Mason, "Autobiography," 250; Sagendorph, *Mason,* 162-68.

17. Sagendorph, *Mason,* 162-68.

18. Ibid., 68-69, 78, 175-77, 255, 379; Mason, "Autobiography," 248-58.

19. Sagendorph, *Mason*, 147, 175; George N. Fuller, *Messages of the Governors of Michigan* (Lansing: Michigan Historical Commission, 1925), I, 121-290.

20. Fuller, *Messages of the Governors*, 125-39, 158-70.

21. Sagendorph, *Mason*, 191-95.

22. Ibid., 195-203 (quotation on p. 198).

23. Ibid., 202.

24. Ibid., 202-23; Mason, "Autobiography," 249.

25. Sagendorph, *Mason*, 232-33.

26. Ibid., 234-58; Fuller, *Messages of the Governors*, 158-69.

27. John Denis Haeger, *John Jacob Astor: Business and Finance in the Early Republic* (Detroit: Wayne State University Press, 1991), 205-21; Herman J. Viola, *Thomas L. McKenney: Architect of America's Early Indian Policy, 1816-1830* (Chicago: Swallow Press, 1974), 21-70.

28. For a description of the Erie Canal, and its impact, see Nathan Miller, *The Enterprise of a Free People: Aspects of Economic Development in New York State during the Canal Period, 1792-1838* (Ithaca: Cornell University Press, 1962); and Ronald E. Shaw, *Canals for a Nation: The Canal Era in the United States, 1790-1860* (Lexington: University Press of Kentucky, 1990). An old but useful study is Alvin F. Harlow, *Old Towpaths: The Story of the American Canal Era* (New York: D. Appleton and Co., 1926).

29. George Rogers Taylor, *The Transportation Revolution, 1815-1860* (New York: Harper & Row, 1951), 32-37; Madeline S. Waggoner, *The Long Haul West: The Great Canal Era, 1817-1850* (New York: G. P. Putnam's Sons, 1958), 32, 100, 180-81, 271-72.

30. Dunbar and May, *Michigan*, 189-90; Cooley, *Michigan*, 203; and Sagendorph, *Mason*, 92; Frank Woodford, *Yankees in Wonderland* (Detroit: Wayne State University Press, 1951), 13-20; Ronald Shaw, "Michigan Influences upon the Formative Years of the Erie Canal," *Michigan History* 37 (March 1953), 1-19.

31. Julius Rubin, *Canal or Railroad? Imitation and Innovation in the Response to the Erie Canal in Philadelphia, Baltimore, and Boston* (Philadelphia: American Philosophical Society, 1961); and Reginald C. McGrane, *Foreign Bondholders and American State Debts* (New York: Macmillan, 1935).

32. Hill, "George Mason," 361-64.

33. Harold M. Dorr, *The Michigan Constitutional Convention of 1835-36* (Ann Arbor: University of Michigan Press, 1940), 394, 479.

34. Fuller, *Messages of the Governors*, 169, 192.

35. Ibid., 194-95.

36. Ibid., 170; Robert J. Parks, *Democracy's Railroads: Public Enterprise in Jacksonian Michigan* (Port Washington, N. Y.: Kennikat Press, 1972), 71-72.

37. Cooley, *Michigan*, 280; Parks, *Democracy's Railroads*, 39-41, 84-87, 91.

38. Fuller, *Messages of the Governors*, 196-97; Parks, *Democracy's Railroads*, 84-86; Dunbar and May, *Michigan*, 271-77.

39. Mason, "Autobiography," 255-56; Sagendorph, *Mason*, 293-94, 327, 339-40.

40. Parks, *Democracy's Railroads*, 186-208; McGrane, *Foreign Bondholders*, 143-67.

41. Dunbar and May, *Michigan*, 274; Ronald P. Formisano, *The Birth of Mass Political Parties: Michigan, 1827-1861* (Princeton, N. J.: Princeton University Press, 1971), 117; Gene Schabath, "Cross-state Canal Stayed Just a Dream," *The Detroit News*, April 24, 1995, B3.

42. Parks, *Democracy's Railroads*, 134-38; Schabath, "Cross-state Canal," B3.

43. Parks, *Democracy's Railroads*, 85, 91-117.

44. Ibid., 225.

45. Ibid., 118-31, 224.

46. Ibid., 134, 138-39.

47. Fuller, *Messages of the Governors*, 284.

48. Parks, *Democracy's Railroads*, 219-33.

49. Ibid., 63-90, 120-22, 154-85; Fuller, *Messages of the Governors*, 194-95.

50. Parks, *Democracy's Railroads*, 120-23, 128, 162-67.

51. Ibid., 92-94.

52. Ibid., 125, 224.

53. Taylor, *The Transportation Revolution*, 21, 36, 51; Clifford Thies, "Infrastructure's Forgotten Failures," *The Free Market* 10 (July 1994), 6; Sagendorph, *Mason*, 397, 404-13.

54. Mason, "Autobiography," 256; McGrane, *Foreign Bondholders*, 62-81; James W. Livingood, *The Philadelphia-Baltimore Trade Rivalry, 1780-1860* (Harrisburg: The Pennsylvania Historical and Museum Commission, 1947); and Hemans, *Mason*, 508-09.

55. Fuller, *Messages of the Governors*, 284, 382-86, 512-13.

56. Ibid., 516.

57. Cooley, *Michigan*, 290.

58. Fuller, *Messages of the Governors*, II, 45.

59. Willis F. Dunbar, *All Aboard! A History of Railroads in Michigan* (Grand Rapids, Mich.: Eerdmans Publishing Co., 1969), 29-56.

60. Cooley, *Michigan,* 291-93.

61. Grand Rapids *Enquirer,* October 9, 1850. See also Dunbar and May, *Michigan,* 366; Milo M. Quaife and Sidney Glazer, *Michigan: From Primitive Wilderness to Industrial Commonwealth* (New York: Prentice Hall, 1948)), 188.

Chapter Three

1. Rolland H. Maybee, *Michigan's White Pine Era* (Lansing: Michigan Department of State, 1988), 11. By 1897, Michigan had already cut more than 160 billion board feet of pine, and had only 6 billion board feet left standing.

2. Bruce Catton, *Michigan: A History* (New York: W. W. Norton & Co., 1984), 71-72. Scholars have debated how seriously the Tiffin report retarded settlement to Michigan. For differing views, see Madison Kuhn, "Tiffin, Morse, and the Reluctant Pioneer," Michigan History, 50 (June 1966), 111-38; and Bernard C. Peters, "The Remaking of an Image: The Propaganda Campaign to Attract Settlers to Michigan, 1815-1840," *The Geographical Survey,* 3 (January 1974), 25-32.

3. Richard G. Wood, *A History of Lumbering in Maine, 1820-1861* (Orono, Maine: University of Maine Press, 1935); and Burton W. Folsom, Jr., *Urban Capitalists: Entrepreneurs and City Growth in Pennsylvania's Lackawanna and Lehigh Regions, 1800-1920* (Baltimore: Johns Hopkins University Press, 1981).

4. Barbara E. Benson, *Logs and Lumber: The Development of Lumbering in Michigan's Lower Peninsula, 1837-1870* (Mount Pleasant, Mich.: Clarke Historical Library, 1989), 64-94, 108, 136-38; Maybee, *Michigan's White Pine Era,* 14, 25.

5. Benson, *Logs and Lumber,* 19-36.

6. Thomas M. Cooley, *Michigan: A History of Governments* (Boston: Houghton, Mifflin and Co., 1892), 289-92.

7. Burton W. Folsom, Jr., *The Myth of the Robber Barons,* third edition (Herndon, Va.: Young America's Foundation, 1996), 17-39; Burton W. Folsom, Jr., *The Progressive Era in Nebraska* (forthcoming). Michigan did give a ten cent per bushel salt subsidy in 1859, but repealed the law after about one year.

8. The importance of local control is stressed by Jeremy W. Kilar, *Michigan's Lumbertowns: Lumbermen and Laborers in Saginaw, Bay City and Muskegon, 1870-1905* (Detroit: Wayne State University Press, 1990). See also Maybee, *Michigan's White Pine Era,* 19-34; Benson, *Logs and Lumber,* 150-51.

9. Lewis C. Reimann, *When Pine Was King* (Ann Arbor: University of Michigan

Press, 1952); Willis F. Dunbar and George S. May, *Michigan: A History of the Wolverine State* (Grand Rapids, Mich.: Eerdmans Publishing Co., 1980), 465-71.

10. Martin D. Lewis, *Lumberman from Flint: The Michigan Career of Henry H. Crapo, 1855-1869* (Detroit: Wayne State University Press, 1958), 13-21. A helpful book by Crapo's grandson is Henry Howland Crapo II, *The Story of Henry Howland Crapo, 1804-1869* (Boston: Thomas Todd Co., 1933). The Crapo papers are available on microfilm in the Bentley Library at the University of Michigan. They are well organized and helpful, but Crapo's handwriting is hard to read. For specific quotations I will often rely on the Lewis and Crapo books.

11. Crapo, *Crapo*, 118-21; Lewis, *Lumberman from Flint*, 19-25. Henry Crapo originally sent his son William to Michigan to survey the lands.

12. Lewis, *Lumberman from Flint*, 22-29, 38-39, 50-58 (quotation on p. 54).

13. Ibid., 54.

14. Ibid., 37, 45, 50.

15. Ibid., 55-56.

16. Ibid., 73, 123.

17. Ibid., 73.

18. Ibid., 115, 132-35 (quotation on p. 132). Technically, Crapo's son William became the president of the Pere Marquette Railroad. Henry felt the need to "conciliate these careful, conservative investors of New Bedford, who habituated to the hazards of the whale fishery, felt very much at sea in adventuring on a railroad in the forests of Michigan." See Crapo, *Crapo*, 169-71 (quotation on p. 169).

19. Lewis, *Lumberman from Flint*, 120-21, 126-28, 188, 239 (quotations on pp. 188, 239).

20. George N. Fuller, *Messages of the Governors of Michigan* (Lansing: Michigan Historical Commission, 1926), II, 515-18; Carl Crow, *The City of Flint Grows Up* (New York: Harper Brothers, 1945), 21-22.

21. Fuller, *Messages of the Governors*, II, 518-20; Crapo, *Crapo*, 253-57.

22. Lewis, *Lumberman from Flint*, 217-18.

23. Crapo, *Crapo*, 254-58 (quotation on p. 258).

24. Ibid., 254-58; Lewis, *Lumberman from Flint*, 221-24, 235-41. A good brief account of Crapo's vetoes is in George M. Blackburn, "Michigan," in James C. Mohr, ed., *Radical Republicans in the North: State Politics during Reconstruction* (Baltimore: Johns Hopkins University Press, 1976), 123-25. In 1870 and 1871, the supreme court in Michigan handed down two separate decisions that upheld Crapo's interpretation of the Constitution of 1850.

25. Fuller, *Messages of the Governors*, II, 608.

26. Crapo, *Crapo*, 139, 162; Lewis, *Lumberman from Flint*, 201-02, 241.

27. Lewis, *Lumberman from Flint*, 251.

28. Ibid., 241; Bernard A. Weisberger, *The Dream Maker: William C. Durant, Founder of General Motors* (Boston: Little, Brown, and Co., 1979), 23.

29. Lewis, *Lumberman from Flint*, 89-90.

30. Weisberger, *The Dream Maker*, 17-18.

31. Ibid., 11, 18.

32. Ibid., 19, 21-22.

33. The relative who opened his house to the Durants was Dr. James C. Willson, Willie's uncle. Dr. Willson's wife and Willie's mother were sisters. Lawrence R. Gustin, *Billy Durant: Creator of General Motors* (Grand Rapids, Mich.: Eerdmans Publishing Co., 1973), 30.

34. Weisberger, *The Dream Maker*, 27-30, 34-35.

35. Ibid., 39-43; Gustin, *Billy Durant*, 17-19.

36. Gustin, *Billy Durant*, 17-19; Weisberger, *The Dream Maker*, 41.

37. Weisberger, *The Dream Maker*, 41-43 (quotation on p. 43).

38. Gustin, *Billy Durant*, 19-20.

39. Ibid., 20-21.

40. Ibid., 22-25 (quotation on p. 23).

41. Weisberger, *The Dream Maker*, 45-46.

42. Ibid., 46-47.

43. Gustin, *Billy Durant*, 42-48 (quotation on p. 43).

44. Ibid, 42-48; Crow, *The City of Flint Grows Up*, 34-35; Weisberger, *The Dream Maker*, 47-53 (quotation on p. 52).

45. Crow, *The City of Flint Grows Up*, 77; Weisberger, *The Dream Maker*, 50, 53; Dunbar and May, *Michigan*, 469.

46. Weisberger, *The Dream Maker*, 53-54.

47. Gustin, *Billy Durant*, 41-42.

48. A good article on Durant's switch from carriages to cars is James J. Flink and Glenn A. Niemeyer, "The General of General Motors," *American Heritage* 24 (August 1973), 11-16, 86-91.

49. Ibid., 14, 16; Gustin, *Billy Durant*, 75-77; Weisberger, *The Dream Maker*, 92-93, 96-99; Arthur Pound, *The Turning Wheel: The Story of General Motors through Twenty-Five Years, 1908-1933* (Garden City, N. Y.: Doubleday, 1934), 68-90.

50. Alfred P. Sloan, Jr., *My Years with General Motors* (Garden City, N. Y.: Doubleday, 1964), 4; Gustin, *Billy Durant*, 71-73, 81-82; Flink and Niemeyer, "The General of General Motors," 11, 86.

51. Allan Nevins, *Ford: The Times, the Man, the Company* (New York: Charles Scribner's Sons, 1954), 412-14; Flink and Niemeyer, "The General of General Motors," 86-87.

52. Weisberger, *The Dream Maker*, 139; Sloan, *General Motors*, 4, 7; Flink and Niemeyer, "The General of General Motors," 87.

53. Gustin, *Billy Durant*, 145-80; Weisberger, *The Dream Maker*, 153-201.

54. Alfred P. Sloan, Jr., *Adventures of a White Collar Man* (Garden City, N. Y.: Doubleday, 1941), 103-08, 127-28 (quotation on pp. 103-04). See also Weisberger, *The Dream Maker*, 209-13; Gustin, *Billy Durant*, 199, 202.

55. Crow, *The City of Flint Grows Up*, 84; Gustin, *Billy Durant*, 94-95, 178.

56. For differing views of Durant's "genius," see J. Patrick Wright, *On a Clear Day You Can See General Motors* (Grosse Pointe, Mich.: Wright Enterprises, 1979), 184-88; and Alfred D. Chandler, Jr., and Stephen Salsbury, *Pierre S. duPont and the Making of the Modern Corporation* (New York: Harper and Row, 1971).

57. Weisberger, *The Dream Maker*, 275-333; Flink and Niemeyer, "The General of General Motors," 88.

58. Weisberger, *The Dream Maker*, 335-63; Gustin, *Billy Durant*, 233-49; Flink and Niemeyer, "The General of General Motors," 90-91.

Chapter Four

1. Murray Campbell and Harrison Hatton, *Herbert H. Dow: Pioneer in Creative Chemistry* (New York: Appleton-Century-Crofts, 1951), 3.

2. Herbert Dow briefly describes his father's influence in a letter he wrote in 1928, in the Post Street Archives (hereafter PSA), Midland, Michigan, doc. #87001. A good secondary account is Don Whitehead, *The Dow Story: The History of the Dow Chemical Company* (New York: McGraw-Hill, 1968), 19.

3. See "The Agreement between William Chisholm and Joseph H. Dow," December 20, 1877, PSA, doc. # 87002. See also Whitehead, *The Dow Story*, 19-21; Campbell and Hatton, *Herbert Dow*, 8-11.

4. Whitehead, *The Dow Story*, 20.

5. Campbell and Hatton, *Herbert Dow*, 11-12.

6. Whitehead, *The Dow Story*, 21.

7. Ibid., 24; Campbell and Hatton, *Herbert Dow*, 15-19.

8. Campbell and Hatton, *Herbert Dow*, 28.

9. Whitehead, *The Dow Story*, 29.

10. Ibid., 31-32.

11. Campbell and Hatton, *Herbert Dow*, 41-42.

12. Ibid., 31-36.

13. For good summaries of the bleach war, see Campbell and Hatton, *Herbert Dow*, 55-60; and Whitehead, *The Dow Story*, 40, 53-54, 67. An excellent new book is E. N. Brandt, *Growth Company: Dow Chemical's First Century* (East Lansing: Michigan State University Press, 1997).

14. Campbell and Hatton, *Herbert Dow*, 58.

15. Ibid., 60.

16. For helpful accounts of the bromine war, see Campbell and Hatton, *Herbert Dow*, 72-78; and Whitehead, *The Dow Story*, 55-56, 59-61, 66, 69, 71.

17. Herbert Dow, "The Dow Chemical Company's Experience with German Competitors," PSA, doc. # 200047. See also Dow's description in an untitled paper, PSA, doc. # 270065.

18. Dow's account of the Jacobsohn episode is in Dow, "The Dow Chemical Company's Experience with German Competitors," 1-3.

19. "German Yellow Dog Fund," from *The American Economist*, February 4, 1921, PSA, doc. # 210156.

20. Dow, "The Dow Chemical Company's Experience with German Competitors." See also "German Bromides," PSA, doc. # 080017; and Whitehead, *The Dow Story*, 59-61.

21. Campbell and Hatton, *Herbert Dow*, 76.

22. Ibid., 75.

23. Ibid., 76.

24. Dow gives a full account of the price-cutting war in "Statement of Mr. Herbert H. Dow, of the Dow Chemical Company, Midland, Michigan," to the Federal Trade Commission, Detroit, July 22, 1915, pp. 2-8. See also Whitehead, *The Dow Story*, 62.

25. Campbell and Hatton, *Herbert Dow*, 76-77.

26. Ibid., 63-71; Whitehead, *The Dow Story*, 68.

27. Campbell and Hatton, *Herbert Dow*, 71.

28. Whitehead, *The Dow Story*, 58.

29. Ibid., 96.

30. Ibid., 76; Campbell and Hatton, *Herbert Dow*, 69.

31. Whitehead, *The Dow Story*, 20.

32. Two useful accounts of the dye business are Campbell and Hatton, *Herbert Dow*, 102-08; Whitehead, *The Dow Story*, 81-82, 89.

33. Campbell and Hatton, *Herbert Dow*, 104.

34. Ibid., 104. The textile producers also approached DuPont and other chemical companies with pleas for more experiments to make dyes.

35. Ibid., 106-07.

36. "Statement of Herbert Dow" to the Federal Trade Commission, 1.

37. Campbell and Hatton, *Herbert Dow*, 107-08.

38. "Statement of Herbert Dow" to the Federal Trade Commission, 2.

39. Campbell and Hatton, *Herbert Dow*, 127.

40. Dow, "The Dow Chemical Company's Experience with German Competitors," 1.

41. Two useful articles on Dow and magnesium are Allen Shoenfield, "Chemists Make Metal of Brine," *The Detroit News*, June 23, 1921; and Herbert Dow, "Notes Dictated by Mr. Dow for Talk at Stockholders' Meeting, June 23, 1920, but Not Used," PSA, doc. # 200052.

42. Campbell and Hatton, *Herbert Dow*, 159.

43. The story of the iodine cartel is in Whitefield, *The Dow Story*, 104-05, 131-33. Iodine had the potential to eliminate the knock in gasoline, but, with the success of ethylene dibromide, iodine ended up having other uses, as a medicine for example.

Chapter Five

1. Scott Bruce and Bill Crawford, *Cerealizing America: The Unsweetened story of American Breakfast Cereal* (Boston: Faber and Faber, 1995), xv. The Bruce and Crawford book is well-written and informative.

2, Ibid. 10; Gerald Carson, *Cornflake Crusade* (New York: Rinehart & Co., 1957), 77-80.

3. Richard W. Schwartz, *John Harvey Kellogg, M.D.* (Nashville: Southern Publishing Association, 1970), 17-18; Carson, *Cornflake Crusade*, 74-76, 82; Bruce and Crawford, *Cerealizing America*, 11-12.

4. Bruce and Crawford, *Cerealizing America*, 12-13; Carson, *Cornflake Crusade*, 83.

5. Schwarz, *John Harvey Kellogg*, 26-36.

6. Bruce and Crawford, *Cerealizing America*, 14; Larry B. Massie and Peter J.

Schmitt, *Battle Creek: the Place Behind the Product* (Woodland Hills, Calif.: Windsor Publications, 1984), 8.

7. Schwarz, *John Harvey Kellogg*, 82-83; Carson, *Cornflake Crusade*, 113-14.

8. Bruce and Crawford, *Cerealizing America*, 17; Carson, *Cornflake Crusade*, 233, 234, 241.

9. Schwarz, *John Harvey Kellogg*, 88-89; Bruce and Crawford, *Cerealizing America*, 18.

10. Schwarz, *John Harvey Kellogg*, 111-13; Bruce and Crawford, *Cerealizing America*, 16-17.

11. Bruce and Crawford, *Cerealizing America*, 17-18.

12. Horace B. Powell, *The Original Has This Signature—W.K. Kellogg* (Englewood Cliffs, N.J.: Prentice-Hall, 1956), 57, 84.

13. Ibid., 26, 32-33, 35; Carson, *Cornflake Crusade*, 87.

14. Powell, *W.K. Kellogg*, 59-61, 68; Carson, *Cornflake Crusade*, 87.

15. Carson, *Cornflake Crusade*, 141-43; Powell, *W.K. Kellogg*, 60, 73, 95.

16. Carson, *Cornflake Crusade*, 87; Powell, *W.K. Kellogg*, 64.

17. Bruce and Crawford, *Cerealizing America*, 20-21.

18. Powell, *W.K. Kellogg*, 90-95.

19. Ibid. , 92; Bruce and Crawford, *Cerealizing America*, 22-23.

20. Bruce and Crawford, *Cerealizing America*, 24-30, 50, 52.

21. Powell, *W.K. Kellogg*, 103.

22. Ibid., 299.

23. Ibid., 110; Carson, *Cornflake Crusade*, 198-99.

24. Powell, *W.K. Kellogg*, 121.

25. Ibid., 132-34. An excellent brief summary of the career of Will Kellogg is in Joseph J. Fucini and Suzy Fucini, *Entrepreneurs: The Men and Women Behind Famous Brand Names and How They Made It* (Boston: G. K. Hall & Co., 1985), 155-57.

26. Powell, *W.K. Kellogg*, 133.

27. Ibid., 132-36; Frank Rowsome, Jr., *They Laughed When I Sat Down* (New York: McGraw-Hill, 1959), 60, 62, 65-67.

28. Powell, *W.K. Kellogg*, 118.

29. Ibid., 124. The loan that Kellogg received was for $30,000, which was enough to put him back in business.

30. Ibid., 125. I would like to thank James McQuiston for identifying Charles W. Post as Kellogg's nemesis.

31. Ibid., 125-26.

32. Ibid., 182.

33. Fucini, *Entrepreneurs*, 155-57; Bruce and Crawford, *Cerealizing America*, 91, 112-13.

34. Powell, *W.K. Kellogg*, 161-62, 182.

35. Carson, *Cornflake Crusade*, 225-26; Bruce and Crawford, *Cerealizing America*, 57.

36. Powell, *W.K. Kellogg*, 159, 213, 220; Bruce and Crawford, *Cerealizing America*, 57.

37. Powell, *W.K. Kellogg*, 144, 160, 187, 291.

38. Ibid., 160, 165, 167, 172, 291.

39. Ibid., 188, 276-77.

40. Ibid., 303, 314.

41. Ibid., 303-07, 311, 323.

42. Carson, *Cornflake Crusade*, 207-09; Bruce and Crawford, *Cerealizing America*, 53-56.

43. Carson, *Cornflake Crusade*, 229-31, 233-34, 241-43.

44. Ibid., 233, 240-42.

45. Powell, *W.K. Kellogg*, 214-15.

46. Carson, *Cornflake Crusade*, 237, 246-47.

47. Powell, *W.K. Kellogg*, 286-87.

48. Ibid., 286.

Chapter Six

1. Henry Ford, in collaboration with Samuel Crowther, *My Life and Work* (Garden City, N.Y.: Doubleday, 1926), 7,8.

2. Allan Nevins and Frank Ernest Hill, *Ford: Expansion and Challenge, 1915-1933* (New York: Charles Scribner's Sons, 1957), 31-33, 38-41.

3. Ford, *My Life and Work,*, 22-32; Nevins and Hill, *Ford*, 42-141.

4. Nevins and Hill, *Ford*, 142-68.

5. Garet Garrett, *The Wild Wheel*, (New York: Pantheon, 1952), 79.

6. Ford, *My Life and Work*, 35; and Jonathan Hughes, *The Vital Few: The Entrepreneurs and American Economic Progress* (New York: Oxford University Press, 1986).

7. Garrett, *The Wild Wheel*, 171-73; Nevins, *Ford*, 245; Hughes, *The Vital Few*, 309;

Harry Barnard, *Independent Man: The Life of Senator James Couzens* (New York: Charles Scribner's Sons, 1958).

8. Ford, *My Life and Work*, 67; Garrett, *The Wild Wheel*, 61.

9. Harold C. Livesay, *American Made: Men Who Shaped the American Economy* (Boston: Little, Brown, and Co., 1979), 171.

10. Ibid., 176.; Charles Sorensen, *My Forty Years with Ford*, (New York: Norton, 1956), 97-112; Barnard, *Couzens*, 66-69.

11. Nevins and Hill, *Ford*, 388; Hughes, *The Vital Few*, 292.

12. Hughes, *The Vital Few*, 292.

13. Garrett, *The Wild Wheel*, 59; Hughes, *The Vital Few*, 292.

14. Ford, *My Life and Work*, 145, 161-62; Peter Collier and David Horowitz, *The Fords: An American Epic* (New York: Summit Books, 1987), 64; Hughes, *The Vital Few*, 327.

15. Garrett, *The Wild Wheel*, 58-64, 86-87.

16. Collier and Horowitz, *The Fords*, 63; Ford, *My Life and Work*, 145.

17. Ford, *My Life and Work*, 112; Collier and Horowitz, *The Fords*, 65-67.

18. Ford, *My Life and Work*, 126-29, 145.

19. Ibid., 70, 126-27, 145, 147.

20. Samuel Marquis, *Henry Ford: An Interpretation* (Boston: Little, Brown, and Co., 1923), 50; Collier and Horowitz, *The Fords*, 65-68; Nevins and Frank Hill, *Ford:* 332.

21. Collier and Horowitz, *The Fords*, 123; Ford, *My Life and Work*, 145; Garrett, *The Wild Wheel*, 64.

22. Garrett, *The Wild Wheel*, 211; Hughes, *The Vital Few*, 308-09.

23. Nevins and Hill, *Ford*, 116.

24. Horowitz, *The Fords*, 132-34; Garrett, *The Wild Wheel*, 152.

25. Garrett, *The Wild Wheel*, 117.

26. Ibid., 47.

27. Spencer Ervin, *Henry Ford vs. Truman Newberry: The Famous Senate Election Contest* (New York: Richard R. Smith, 1935); Nevins and Hill, *Ford*, 114-42, 301-05.

28. Ford, *My Life and Work*, 8; Henry Ford, *My Philosophy of Industry* (New York: Coward-McCann, 1929), 25, 61.

29. Ford, *My Life and Work*, 108-10; Allan Nevins and Frank Ernest Hill, *Ford: Decline and Rebirth, 1933-1962* (New York: Charles Scribner's Sons, 1963), 407.

30. Scott D. Trostel, *Henry Ford: When I Ran the Railroads* (Fletcher, Ohio: Cam-Tech Publishing, 1989), 95-99, 145-46; Ford, *My Life and Work*, 233.

31. William Greenleaf, *Monopoly on Wheels: Henry Ford and the Selden Automobile Patent* (Detroit: Wayne State University Press, 1961); Allan Nevins, *Ford: The Times, the Man, the Company* (New York: Charles Scribner's Sons, 1954), 284-322; Garrett, *The Wild Wheel*, 74-75.

32. Lincoln Highway Association, *The Lincoln Highway: The Story of a Crusade that Made Transportation History* (New York: Dodd, Mead & Co., 1935), 14-17, 86, 152, 208; Willis F. Dunbar and George S. May, *Michigan: A History of the Wolverine State* (Grand Rapids, Mich.: Eerdmans Publishing Co., 1980), 570-71; Nevins, *Ford*, 484-87.

33. Ford, *My Life and Work*, 184; Nevins and Hill, *Ford, 1915-1933*, 300-23.

34. A critical account of Ford is Keith Sward, *The Legend of Henry Ford* (New York: Rinehart, 1948).

35. Ford, *My Life and Work*, 71; Nevins and Hill, *Ford, 1915-1933*, 409-36.

36. Nevins and Hill, *Ford, 1915-1933*, 416-18.

37. Garrett, *The Wild Wheel*, 173; Nevins and Hill, *Ford, 1933-1962*, 2; Livesay, *American Made*, 176.

38 Sward, *The Legend of Henry Ford*, 199-216.

39. Hughes, *The Vital Few*, 337; Nevins and Hill, *Ford, 1933-1962*, 4.

40. Burton W. Folsom, Jr., *The Myth of the Robber Barons* (Herndon, Va.: Young America's Foundation, 1996), 103-20; Hans Sennholz, *The Great Depression: Will We Repeat It?* (Irvington, N. Y.: Foundation for Economic Education, 1992).

41. Hughes, *The Vital Few*, 347.

42. Sidney Fine, *The Automobile Under the Blue Eagle* (Ann Arbor: University of Michigan Press, 1963), 54, 75-77, 83-85, 94-95; William A. Simonds, *Henry Ford: His Life, His Work, His Genius* (Indianapolis: Bobbs-Merrill, 1943), 241-60; Nevins and Hill, *Ford, 1933-1962*, 17.

43. Harry Bennett, *We Never Called Him Henry* (New York: Fawcett, 1951), 96; Nevins and Hill, *Ford, 1933-1962*, 19.

44. Nevins and Hill, *Ford, 1933-1962*, 21, 38, 41; Garrett, *The Wild Wheel*, 153.

45. Carol Gelderman, *Henry Ford: The Wayward Capitalist* (New York: Dial Press, 1980), 325.

46. U. S. Bureau of the Census, *Historical Statistics of the United States* (Washington: Government Printing Office, 1975), 1107; Roy G. Blakey and Gladys C. Blakey, *The*

Federal Income Tax (London: Longmans, Green and Co., 1940); Folsom, *The Myth of the Robber Barons*, 103-20.

47. Nevins and Hill, *Ford, 1933-1962,* 411-13.

48. Ibid., 413-19.

49. Ford, *My Life and Work*, 255-62.

50. Garrett, *The Wild Wheel,* 146-48.

51. Collier and Horowitz, *The Fords*, 116; Nevins and Hill, *Ford, 1915-1933,* 350, 525.

52. Nevins and Hill, *Ford, 1915-1933*, 514-19; Nevins and Hill, *Ford, 1933-1962,* 152-53; Collier and Horowitz, *The Fords*, 160-62.

53. Collier and Horowitz, *The Fords*, 152-66; Nevins and Hill, *Ford,1933-1962,* 233.

54. Nevins and Hill, *Ford, 1933-1962,* 109-67, 228-51.

55. Ibid., 155.

56. Ibid., 164.

57. Henry Hazlitt, *Economics in One Lesson* (New Rochelle, N. Y.: Arlington House, 1979), 140-53.

58. Garrett, *The Wild Wheel,* 38; Nevins and Hill, *Ford,1933-1962,* 166.

59. Nevins and Hill, *Ford, 1933-1962,* 300-01.

Chapter Seven

1. Garet Garrett, *The Wild Wheel* (New York: Pantheon Books, 1952), 160-61.

2. George Gilder, *Recapturing the Spirit of Enterprise* (San Francisco: ICS Press, 1992), 308. See also Douglas McGregor, *The Human Side of Enterprise* (New York: McGraw-HIll, 1985), for a comparison of different styles of management.

3. Allan Nevins, *Ford: The Times, The Man, The Company* (New York: Charles Scribner's Sons, 1954), 239.

4. Henry Ford, *My Life and Work* (Garden City, N.Y.: Doubleday, 1926), 146.

5. Lawrence R. Gustin, *Billy Durant: Creator of General Motors* (Grand Rapids, Mich.: Eerdmans Publishing Co., 1973), 196.

6. Allan Nevins and Frank Ernest Hill, *Ford: Decline and Rebirth, 1933-1962* (New York: Charles Scribner's Sons, 1963), 41.

7. Garrett, *The Wild Wheel,* 220.

Appendix

1. Irwin Unger, *These United States*, 4th edition (Englewood Cliffs, N. J.: Prentice Hall, 1989), 440.

2. I develop this idea in *The Myth of the Robber Barons: A New Look at the Rise of Big Business in America*, 3rd edition (Herndon, Va.: Young America's Foundation, 1996).

3. Willis F. Dunbar and George S. May, Michigan: *A History of the Wolverine State*, (Grand Rapids, Mich.: Eerdmans Publishing Co., 1980), 279.

4. Bruce A. Rubenstein and Lawrence E. Ziewacz, *Michigan: A History of the Great Lakes State* (Wheeling, Ill.: Harlan Davidson, 1995), 67.

5. Robert Parks, *Democracy's Railroads: Public Enterprise in Jacksonian Michigan* (Port Washington, N. Y.: Kennikat Press, 1972), 233.

6. Folsom, *The Myth of the Robber Barons*, 17-39.

7. Karen Potter-Witter, "Timber Producer Certification in Michigan: Self Regulation vs. State Regulation," Mackinac Center for Public Policy, February 1995.

8. Terry L. Anderson and Donald R. Leal, *Free Market Environmentalism* (Boulder, Colo.: Westview Press, 1991), 51-52.

Index

EMPIRE BUILDERS

Cover design by Eric Norton

Text design by Mary Jo Zazueta
in New Baskerville with display lines
in Goudy Modern MT

Text stock is 50 lb. Royal Antique

Printed and bound by Royal Book,
Norwich, Connecticut

Production Editor: Alex Moore